PLATO

PLATO

•

Julia Annas

A BRIEF
INSIGHT

STERLING

New York / London
www.sterlingpublishing.com

STERLING and the distinctive Sterling logo are registered trademarks of
Sterling Publishing Co., Inc.

Library of Congress Cataloging-in-Publication Data Available

10 9 8 7 6 5 4 3 2 1

Published by Sterling Publishing Co., Inc.
387 Park Avenue South, New York, NY 10016
Published by arrangement with Oxford University Press, Inc.
© 2003 by Julia Annas
Illustrated edition published in 2009 by Sterling Publishing Co., Inc.
Additional text © 2009 Sterling Publishing Co., Inc.
Distributed in Canada by Sterling Publishing
c/o Canadian Manda Group, 165 Dufferin Street
Toronto, Ontario, Canada M6K 3H6

Book design: The DesignWorks Group
Please see picture credits on page 175 for image copyright information.

Manufactured in the United States of America
All rights reserved

Sterling ISBN 978-1-4027-7052-4

For information about custom editions, special sales, premium and
corporate purchases, please contact Sterling Special Sales
Department at 800-805-5489 or specialsales@sterlingpublishing.com.

Frontispiece: Bust of Plato

CONTENTS

•

PLATO

ONE

Arguing with Plato

●

The Jury's Problem

Imagine that you are on a jury, listening to Smith describe how he was set upon and robbed. The details are striking, the account hangs together, and you are completely convinced; you believe that Smith was the victim of a violent crime. This is a true belief; Smith was, in fact, attacked.

Do you *know* that Smith was attacked? This might at first seem like an odd thing to worry about. What better evidence could you have? But you might reflect that this is, after all, a courtroom, and that Smith is making a case which his alleged attacker will then try to counter. Can you be sure that you are convinced because Smith is telling the truth, or might it be the way the case is being presented that is persuading you? If it is the latter, then you might be worried;

In reading Plato, it is important to pay attention to the role of argument. This undated mural painting by Pierre Puvis de Chavannes showing Plato conversing with a student at the Academy hangs in the Boston Public Library.

for then you might have been convinced even if Smith had not been telling the truth. Besides, even if he is telling the truth, is his evidence conclusive as to his being attacked? For all you know, he might have been part of a setup, and it's not as though you had been there and seen it for yourself. And so it can seem quite natural to conclude that you don't actually *know* that Smith was attacked, though you have a belief about it which is true, and no actual reason to doubt its truth.

· · · · ·

THE *THEAETETUS*

The *Theaetetus* is one of Plato's most appealing dialogues, but also one of his most puzzling. In it, Socrates says that he is a midwife like his mother: he draws ideas out of people, before testing them to see whether they hold up to reasoned examination. Refusing to put forward his own ideas about what knowledge is (though displaying sophisticated awareness of the work of other philosophers), he shows faults in all of the accounts of knowledge suggested by young Theaetetus. Pursuing the thought that if you *know* something, you can't be wrong, Theaetetus suggests that knowing might be perceiving; then having a true belief; then, having a true belief and being able to defend or "give an account of" it. All these suggestions fail, and the dialogue leaves us better off only in awareness of our own inability to sustain an account of knowing. Socrates' insistence on arguing only against the positions of others, not for any position of his own, made the dialogue a key one for the Platonic tradition which took Plato's inheritance to be one of seeking truth by questioning those who claim to have it (as Socrates often does in the dialogues)

In the *Theaetetus*, rather than espousing and supporting with philosophical argument his own idea of what knowledge is, Socrates simply refutes the many attempts of the young Theaetetus to define knowledge. Socrates is shown here discussing a philosophical premise with two pupils in a manuscript from the first half of the thirteenth century.

rather than by making his own philosophical claims. Others, noting that in other dialogues we find positive, ambitious claims about the nature of knowledge, thought of the *Theaetetus* as clearing away only accounts of knowledge that Plato took to be mistaken. Socrates here, the midwife of others' ideas who has no "children" of his own, seems very different from the Socrates of other dialogues such as the

The Areopagus (Hill of Ares), the original four-hundred-member supreme tribunal of Athens (later increased to 501 members), is believed to have met in the open air on this rocky hill in Athens.

Republic, who puts forward positive ideas quite confidently. Readers have to come to their own conclusions about this (some ancient and modern solutions are discussed in Chapter 3).

• • • • •

In his dialogue *Theaetetus* Plato raises this issue. What can knowledge be, young Theaetetus asks, other than true belief? After all, if you have a true belief you are not making any mistakes. But Theaetetus is talking to Socrates (of whom more in Chapter 2) and, as often, the older man finds a problem. For persuading people in public is something that can be skillfully done. He means the skill of what we would call lawyers, although he is talking about a system in which there are no professional lawyers. The victim had to present his own case, though many people hired professional speechwriters, especially since they had to convince a jury of not 12 but 501 members.

• • • • •

HOW WE REFER TO PLATO'S WORKS

In 1578 the publisher Henri Etienne, the Latin form of whose surname is Stephanus, produced the first printed edition of Plato's works in Paris. The new technology enabled a much greater number of people than hitherto to read Plato. And for the first time it became possible to refer precisely to passages within dialogues, since readers were for the first time using the same pagination. We still refer to the page on which the passage appeared in Stephanus's edition (for example, 200), together with one of the letters *a* to *e*, which served to divide the page into five areas from top to bottom. "Stephanus numbers" are printed in the margins of most Plato texts and translations, and a reference such as "200e" enables readers to find a passage no matter what the pagination of the book they are using.

• • • • •

Socrates continues:

> *SOCRATES:* These men, at any rate, persuade by means of their expertise, and they don't teach people, but get them to have whatever beliefs they wish. Or do you think that there are any teachers so clever as to teach the truth about what happened adequately, in the short time

allowed, to people who weren't there when others were robbed of their property or violently attacked?

THEAETETUS: No, I don't think they could at all, but I think they could persuade them.

SOCRATES: And by persuading them don't you mean getting them to have a belief?

THEAETETUS: Of course.

SOCRATES: Well, when a jury has been persuaded fairly about something about which you could only have knowledge if you were an eyewitness, not otherwise, while they judge from what they've heard and get a true belief, haven't they then judged without knowledge, though they were persuaded of what's correct, since they made a good judgment?

THEAETETUS: Absolutely.

SOCRATES: But look, if true belief and knowledge were the same thing, then an excellent juryman wouldn't have a correct belief without knowledge. As it is, the two appear to be distinct.

(Theaetetus 201a–c)

This sounds convincing, indeed perhaps blindingly obvious. But, like the jury, we can raise the question of whether we should be convinced. Why *don't* the jury know that Smith was robbed?

Socrates challenges Theaetetus in his attempt to provide a definition of knowledge, using the example of a trial jury being persuaded to adopt a belief, and then judging based on that belief. In this Jean-Léon Gérôme painting from 1861, the courtesan Phryne stands trial for profaning a ceremony dedicated to the goddesses Demeter and Persephone.

What Is Required for Knowledge?

One reason put forward by Plato for the claim that the jury lack knowledge is that they have been persuaded, by someone whose main aim it is to get them to believe what he wants them to believe. In this case he has persuaded them of the truth, but we may think that he would have been able to persuade them even if his story hadn't been true. At first this worry may seem far-fetched: if you have acquired a true belief in a certain way, why worry that you *might have been* persuaded of something false in that same way? How can what didn't happen cast doubt on what did? But, in fact, this worry about the power of persuasion is serious, because it casts doubt on the route by which the belief is acquired. If it is a route by which I can acquire false beliefs as readily as true ones, then it cannot guarantee me only true beliefs. And this does raise a doubt in most people's minds that a belief that I have acquired by that route could amount to knowledge.

Another reason put forward in the passage is that the sort of fact the jury have been persuaded of, namely that Smith was attacked, is not the sort of fact that you could have knowledge of anyway unless you had been there and seen it for yourself. However convinced we are that Smith is telling the truth, all we are getting is a version that is second-hand, and conveyed by an entirely different kind of route from Smith's own. He experienced and saw the robbery; we are only being told about it. However vivid the telling, it's still just a telling; only somebody who was there and saw it can have knowledge of it. Again, this may at first seem far-fetched. If we limit knowledge to what we can actually experience firsthand for ourselves, then there won't be much that we can know; nothing that we read or hear secondhand will count. Yet there is a powerful thought being appealed to here, one that can be expressed by saying that nobody else can know things for you or on your behalf. Knowledge requires that you acquire the relevant belief for yourself. What it is to acquire a belief for yourself will differ depending on the kind of belief it is, but with the belief that Smith was robbed the only way you can acquire it for yourself with no intermediary is, it seems, to be there yourself and actually see it.

A Problem for Us

Plato has given us two kinds of reason for rejecting the idea that the jury's true belief could amount to knowledge. Both are strong, but how well do they go together? The problem with persuasion was that it turned out to be

a route that could not guarantee that the beliefs we acquired from someone else would be true. But for this to be a problem with *persuasion* there has to be the possibility of a route of this kind that did have such a guarantee. Socrates complains that the victim has to convince the jury in too short a time, and in circumstances that are too emotional and fraught, for their acquisition of beliefs to be the right kind for knowledge. This complaint is pointless unless there could be a way of acquiring beliefs that didn't have these disadvantages—say, one where there were no time constraints, and each member of the jury could examine witnesses and victim as much as they required to satisfy every last scruple. So it looks as though we are assuming that there is a way of conveying beliefs that could amount to knowledge, though it isn't persuasion.

The second point, however, suggested that *no* way of conveying beliefs, however careful and scrupulous, could amount to knowledge, since any belief conveyed to you from another will be secondhand, and thus something that you cannot know, because you cannot know it for yourself. Relying on someone else's testimony, however sound, is never the same as experiencing the fact for yourself.

The problem now is that the second objection seems to conflict with the first. The second supposes that knowledge cannot be conveyed, but must be acquired by each person in their own case; but the first found fault with persuasion in a way suggesting that there *could* be a way of acquiring

Plato. Socrates.

a belief from someone else which would amount to knowledge, so that knowledge *is* conveyable.

The Reader Comes In

At this point the reader is forced to think for herself about the passage, and about what Plato is doing. The simplest response would be to conclude that Plato has given Socrates mutually conflicting demands on knowledge because Plato is himself confused; he just hasn't noticed that he is requiring knowledge to be both conveyable and not conveyable. Unsympathetic readers may stop at this point.

We might probe a little further, however. For one thing, Socrates in this dialogue repeatedly stresses that he is not putting forward positions of his own, only arguing against those of others. He produces two objections to Theaetetus's suggestion that true belief might amount to knowledge. Each is powerful against that suggestion. Do we have to suppose that Plato, the author, was unaware that these objections run up against each other? Not necessarily (and if we do not have to suppose the author unaware of this, we also do not have to suppose that he intended to portray Socrates as unaware of this problem—though this is a further matter, on which readers may disagree). And given the sophisticated level of argument in the *Theaetetus*, the reasonable course is to suppose that Plato was aware of how these two objections are related.

Why then does Plato not appear to think that it matters? Here we have to take seriously Socrates' stress in the dialogue that he is only arguing

The reader of the *Theaetetus* must consider whether Plato himself knew that he has given Socrates mutually conflicting demands on knowledge and whether Plato intended that Socrates realize that as well. Plato, who was a student of Socrates', is shown here with his teacher in this English manuscript illumination from the thirteenth century.

against the views of others. This does not mean that he has no ideas on the subject himself, but it does mean that the point of the dialogue is not to put these forward. The problem we find when we reflect on Socrates' two grounds for rejecting Theaetetus's suggestion doesn't undermine the conclusion that that suggestion won't do; they do show that when we, or Plato, are working on a positive account of knowledge we need to be aware of this problem.

In another dialogue, the *Meno*, we find the claim that knowledge is teachable (87b–c), where this is a firmly accepted point. But it is also in the *Meno* that we find one of Plato's most famous ideas, that knowledge is really a sort of "recollection." Socrates engages in a conversation with a boy who knows no geometry, taking him through a geometrical proof which, though simple to follow, contains a step that the boy will find counterintuitive. Having walked him through the proof, Socrates says (85c) that the boy is now in the state of having true beliefs on the subject, but "if someone asks him these same things many times and in many ways, you know that in the end he will have knowledge about them as accurate as anyone's." Socrates has taught the boy in the sense of presenting the proof to him in such a way that the boy can come to have knowledge of it for himself. The boy will not actually have knowledge until he has done something for himself—making the effort to understand the proof. The boy has to come to know the proof for himself, because only he can come to understand it for himself. Socrates can't do that. But Socrates can convey knowledge in that he can convey the proof to the boy in a way that will enable the boy to make the effort for himself. Hence we can see how knowledge can be teachable while it is still true that knowledge is something each person can achieve only for himself. In a further move, Plato calls this recollection; for when the boy comes to understand the proof, Plato holds that his soul has come to recollect knowledge

In the *Meno*, another of Plato's dialogues, Socrates takes a young boy through a geometric proof in such a way that the boy can understand and have knowledge of it himself. This detail of an illustration at the beginning of Euclid's *Elementa* (1309–16), in the translation attributed to twelfth-century English scholar Adelard of Bath, shows a woman, apparently a geometry teacher, and possibly the personification of geometry, instructing a group of students with a set square, dividers, and a compass.

it had prior to embodiment, and thus prior to the boy's actual experience. Clearly, though, the further step about recollection is not required by the argument itself; it is Plato's bold and exciting way of interpreting the results of the argument.

Arguing with Plato

In many ways, the jury passage in the *Theaetetus* provides a good introduction to Plato's way of writing. We find right away that it is important to pay attention to the way in which Plato writes, particularly to the role of argument in supporting one's own position or attacking those of others. We find also that the reader is drawn into the argument herself, needing to challenge Plato's arguments even where Socrates in the dialogue easily wins.

The brief mention I have made of the *Meno* argument introduces us to another feature of Plato's writing. In the *Theaetetus*, Plato uses the point that knowledge is conveyable, and also the point that knowledge requires firsthand experience of one's own. If we follow this through with an everyday example, like the jury's judgment about the crime, we find problems. In the *Meno* we find both points in a context in which they are not in conflict. But the context there is a geometrical proof—an example of knowledge that is very different from the jury's judgment. A geometrical proof is something articulated, abstract, and far removed from everyday experience. There is something substantial to understand, and to convey. It is no accident that when Plato struggles with the concept of knowledge, he tends to conclude that what meets his standards for knowledge is far more restricted than the range of things we normally assume that we know. If we think about the differences between the jury example and a geometrical proof, we can see why he tends to do this. For example, the notion of understanding has less scope with an everyday example in which knowledge just comes down to seeing the crime.

Plato is perhaps best known for what is often called the "Theory of Forms," a set of striking claims about what is real and what we can know. Forms, of which we shall see more, do not figure in the *Meno* or *Theaetetus*, but we can detect in these works lines of thought that make Plato's claims about Forms, when we encounter them, more understandable.

Plato writes in a way which involves us in argument with him. He also puts forward philosophical claims that have seldom been matched

A geometrical proof, in contrast to a jury's judgment, is articulated, abstract, and far removed from everyday experience. Nino Pisano's allegory of geometry with Euclid at his desk is shown in this marble panel from the east side of the lower basement of the bell tower at the Museo dell'Opera del Duomo in Florence, Italy.

for their boldness, and for the imaginative manner in which they are expressed. (The idea that knowledge is "recollection" is one of the most famous of these.) Interpretations of Plato tend to overemphasize one of these aspects at the expense of the other. At times, he has been read as interested solely in engagement with the reader, and distanced from any positive ideas. At other times, he has been read as a bold theorist striding dogmatically ahead, indifferent to argument. What is difficult and also rewarding to bear in mind about Plato is that he is intensely concerned both with argument and with bold ideas, in a way that is subtle and hard to capture without simplification. This introduction to Plato does not pretend either to cover all of Plato's ideas or to provide a recipe for interpreting him, but rather aims to introduce you to engagement with Plato in a way that will, I hope, lead you to persist.

TWO

Plato's Name, and Other Matters

●

Name or Nickname?

Plato's name was probably Plato. The "probably" may surprise you; how can there be any doubt? Plato's writings have come down to us firmly under that name. But within the ancient biographical tradition there is a surprisingly substantial minor tradition according to which "Plato" was a nickname which stuck, while the philosopher's real name was Aristocles. This is credible; Plato's paternal grandfather was called Aristocles, and it was a common practice to call the eldest son after the father's father. We have, however, no independent evidence that Plato was the eldest son. And "Plato" does not appear to be a nickname; it turns up frequently in the period. Further, the explanations we find

Biographies of Plato did not turn up until several generations after the philosopher's death, so their information is unreliable at best. This late-fifteenth-century vellum from *Histoire des Philosophes* depicts Plato at his desk.

for it as a nickname are unconvincing. Because "Plato" suggests *platus*, "broad," we find the suggestion that Plato had been a wrestler known for his broad shoulders, or a writer known for his broad range of styles! Clearly this is just guessing, and we would be wise not to conclude that Plato changed his name or had it changed by others. But then what do we make of the Aristocles stories? We don't know, and can't tell. And this is frustrating. A change of name is an important fact about a person, but this "fact" slips through our fingers.

Our ancient sources about Plato often put us in this position. There are plenty of stories in the ancient biographies of Plato, and frequently they would, if we could rely on them, give us interesting information about Plato as a person. But they nearly always dissolve at a touch.

Facts and Factoids

Plato was born in Athens in 427 BCE and died in 347; we are fairly well informed about his family.

· · · · ·

PLATO'S FAMILY

Both Plato's father, Ariston, and his mother, Perictione, came from old Athenian families. Plato in the *Critias* makes much of his family's descent from the sixth-century statesman Solon, who brought about reforms that put Athens on the road to eventual democracy. Plato had two full brothers, Glaucon and Adeimantus, to whom he allots parts in the *Republic*. After Ariston's death, Perictione married Pyrilampes, who was already the father of a son called Demos (referred to in the *Gorgias*). By Pyrilampes Perictione had a son Antiphon, Plato's half brother, who took up philosophy but quickly lost

Plato was a descendent through his mother of the Athenian statesman lawmaker Solon (ca. 630–ca. 560 BCE), who is shown here with three students in an Arabic manuscript from the first half of the thirteenth century.

interest; he is given the role of narrating the entire conversation of the *Parmenides*. Pyrilampes had strong democratic sympathies (Demos is Greek for "The People"). After Athens's utter defeat in the long-drawn-out Peloponnesian War in 404 BCE, antidemocratic sympathizers brought about a coup and set up a government of thirty (known as the Thirty Tyrants). Perictione's brother Critias and cousin Charmides (both of whom have parts in the *Charmides*) were among them. Plato thus came from a family divided by the civil war. We do not know his own political views, though this has not stopped much speculation about them. It is plausible that he was alienated from the restored democracy by Socrates' execution under it.

$\bullet \ \bullet \ \bullet \ \bullet \ \bullet$

He was regarded as an outstanding philosophical and literary figure from early on, someone around whom stories gathered. However, it was not until several generations had passed that we find what we would call biographies, claiming to give narratives about Plato the individual; in Plato's own time this kind of interest had not developed. By then very few facts about Plato would have been accurately recoverable, but people had begun to want

Although we do not know much about Plato as a person, we do know that he came from a family divided by civil war. Following Athens's defeat by Sparta in the Peloponnesian War, a battle of which is depicted in this ca. 1900 drawing of a naval conflagration in the harbor of Syracuse, his mother's uncle and cousin served in the antidemocratic Thirty Tyrants government, which was established by coup.

to know about the person behind the dialogues (as many of us still do). So we find narratives of Plato's life in which facts about his life are appealed to, often in order to explain why a passage in one of the dialogues says what it does, particularly if there is no other obvious reason for its being there. Thus we find, for example, the claim that Plato went on a journey to Egypt seeking wisdom. There is nothing implausible about this. On the other hand, it is a claim made about many ancient philosophers, particularly in later antiquity with the growth of the idea that Greek wisdom originally came from older, Eastern countries. A passage in the dialogue *Laws* may suggest that Plato had actually seen the stylized Egyptian art which he prefers to the innovations of Greek art, but it does not compel us to that conclusion. We simply do not know whether we have a fact that sheds light on the *Laws* passage, or a factoid created later from that passage.

$$\bullet \ \bullet \ \bullet \ \bullet \ \bullet$$

PLATO ON GREEK AND EGYPTIAN ART

The Athenian in the *Laws*, the dialogue's main speaker, claims that the Greeks have much to learn from the way the Egyptians codified artistic styles and stuck to them, as opposed to the restless craving for originality and new styles marking Greek art of his day.

ATHENIAN: Long ago, it seems, [the Egyptians] recognized this principle of which we are now speaking, namely that the movements and songs that young people in cities practice habitually should be fine ones. They drew up a list of what these are and what they are like and displayed it in the temples. Painters and others who produce any kinds of forms were forbidden to innovate or invent anything nontraditional; and it still is forbidden both to them and in the arts in general. If you look, you will find that things painted or sculpted there ten thousand years ago—and I mean literally ten thousand—are not at all better or worse than what is produced now, but are produced according to the very same skill.

CLEINIAS: It's amazing, what you say.

ATHENIAN: Rather, an exceptional product of legislative and statesmanlike skill.

(Laws 656d–657a)

Whether Plato had traveled to Egypt seeking wisdom and had seen Egyptian art while he was there is a matter of conjecture. We must garner what knowledge we can of the philosopher from his dialogues. In his dialogue *Laws*, for instance, he indicates a preference for the fixed, stylized art of ancient Egypt, shown, for example, in the triad statue of the pharaoh Menkaura, accompanied by the goddess Hathor (on his right) and Parva, the personification of the nome (province) of Diospolis (on his left), over the developing tradition valuing originality of ancient Greece, shown, for example, in the statue of the goddess Eirene (the personification of peace) bearing Plutus (the personification of wealth), a Roman copy after a Greek votive statue by Kephisodotos (ca. 370 BCE).

Some of this suggests that Plato had seen Egyptian art; some suggests that he had not. It does not matter for his point: fixed stylization in art is preferable to a developing tradition valuing originality.

· · · · ·

This matters chiefly in that we do not have independent access to Plato's individual personality as we do for more recent philosophers. In the dialogues he never speaks in his own voice. Whatever we make of this, we cannot evade it by appealing to his life; our views of his life are irrevocably contaminated by the dialogues.

Different Interpretations

Two very differing interpretations are nearly contemporary with Plato himself. His nephew Speusippus, who succeeded him as head of his philosophical school, held that Plato's real father was not Ariston but the god Apollo. A whole corresponding tradition grew up: Plato was born on Apollo's birthday; bees came and sat on his infant lips; his teacher Socrates dreamed of a swan, Apollo's bird, just before meeting Plato. Thinking of Plato as semidivine, alien to us, is not so startling in a world in which great families claimed descent from the gods. It makes the point that would be made in later times by saying that Plato was a genius, somebody altogether out of the ordinary, with talents that transcend the historical circumstances of his birth and upbringing. A similar tradition grew up at some point around Pythagoras. Plato is seen as a more than human figure because of the profundity of his thought and the grandeur of his philosophical conceptions. In this way of looking at him, what matter most are the large pronouncements, rather than arguments and the idea of seeking for the truth. In late antiquity, particularly, Plato was seen as

Plato's nephew Speusippus, who succeeded him as head of Plato's philosophical school, held that Plato's father was not Ariston, but the god Apollo, which led to a tradition of thinking of Plato as semidivine. Apollo, who is the Greek and Roman god of sunlight, prophecy, music, and poetry, is shown here with two muses in an oil on canvas from 1741 by Italian painter Pompeo Batoni.

this kind of towering figure, a superhuman Sage. It is not too hard to find passages in Plato's writings that can inspire this sort of interpretation (particularly in the *Timaeus*).

Probably contemporary with the "son of Apollo" interpretation is the utterly different one found in the so-called Seventh Letter. Among the body of works by Plato that have come down to us are thirteen works purporting to be letters by him to various people. Most of them are of a much later date, but two, the seventh and eighth, contain no definitive anachronisms. The "Seventh Letter" contains what purports to be an autobiographical account by Plato of his early disillusionment with politics, and his attempts, during mysterious visits to the Sicilian city of Syracuse, to persuade the tyrant Dionysius II to submit to constitutional rule. Whether authentic or not, the letter was accepted by many in the ancient world as illuminating Plato's own very idealistic approach to political philosophy. In the last two centuries it has formed the basis for a stronger view, that Plato's impetus to philosophy in the first place was basically political, but this claim is clouded by the persistent authenticity problems. It is a mistake, in any case, to think of it as a psychologically revealing account of an individual experience; it is a rhetorical exercise in defending Plato and Dionysius's opponent Dion, part of a debate of which we have only one side.

We can easily see why the "political" interpretation has seemed more credible and appealing to modern scholars than the "son of Apollo" interpretation, and the former has been widespread for many years. It fits our ways of thinking better to see Plato's philosophy as politically motivated than it does to see it as the work of a transcendent genius (let alone a god!). We should hesitate, however, to claim that the "Seventh Letter" takes us behind the dialogues and gives us the "real" Plato in a way that suggests that his own nephew was wrong. Interpretations of Plato are contested. They were probably contested before he was dead.

Socrates and the Academy

We do have two relatively firm points to grasp in approaching Plato. One is the great influence on him of the Athenian Socrates, and the other is his founding of the Academy, the first philosophical school.

One perspective from which to approach Plato is the great influence that the Athenian philosopher Socrates had on him. This marble bust of Socrates, a Roman copy after a Greek original, is from the fourth century BCE.

SOCRATES

Socrates (about 468–399 BCE) was the son of a stonemason and a midwife. His wife, Xanthippe, has an aristocratic name, and at one point he had the money to serve as a heavy-armed soldier, but by the end of his life he was poor. Plato has Socrates in his *Apology* (*Defense*) ascribe this to his devotion to philosophy, to the neglect of his own affairs. He had three sons; later tradition gives him a second wife, Myrto.

Socrates was tried and executed under the restored democracy in 399. It has often been suspected that he was unpopular because of his association with people who had overthrown the democracy, but the circumstances are unrecoverable. He was found guilty on vague charges of introducing new divinities and corrupting the youth. The first charge probably relates to Socrates' "divine sign" (*daimonion*), which at times held him back.

Socrates quickly became the symbolic figure of the Philosopher, the person devoting his life to philosophical inquiry and willing to die for it. He became a figurehead for many different schools of philosophy; each could find their own ideas or methods in Socrates, who left no writings. He was a controversial person, inspiring both dislike and devotion. The comic dramatist Aristophanes wrote an unpleasant play, *The Clouds*, about him, and he was attacked after his death. Many of his associates produced "Socratic writings" to defend his memory. We have some fragments by his followers Aeschines and Antisthenes, who, along with another follower, Aristippus, went on to develop very different kinds of philosophy. Our main sources, however, are

After his death, Socrates became the symbolic figure of the Philosopher, one willing to die rather than compromise his values, and for this, Plato held him in high esteem, using him as the main figure in most of his dialogues. Italian Baroque painter Salvator Rosa's late-seventeenth-century painting shows Socrates taking poison as ordered by the Athenian court.

Xenophon and Plato. Disputes as to who gives the "truer" picture of Socrates are futile; Socrates was from the first a figure onto whom very different positions could be projected, and the differences between Xenophon's Socrates and Plato's are best seen as differences between Xenophon and Plato.

In Plato's dialogues Plato himself is never a character, and Socrates is usually the chief figure, in dialogue which is sometimes direct and sometimes narrated, by others or by Socrates himself. Plato's Socrates varies enormously between dialogues. Sometimes he is a persistent

Socrates was a controversial figure, inspiring both dislike and devotion. Comic dramatist Aristophanes, shown here in an undated bust portrait, fell into the former camp; his play about Socrates, *The Clouds*, was not flattering.

Socrates left no writings of his own. Our main sources for his ideas and methods are Plato and Greek historian Xenophon (ca. 431–ca. 352 BCE), who is shown here in an engraving by George Cooke published in 1810 in *The Historical Gallery of Portraits and Paintings*.

questioner of others' positions; sometimes he puts forward his own views confidently and at length; sometimes he is merely a bystander. Plato was always inspired by Socrates as the ideal figure of the philosopher, but his views as to what the tasks and methods of philosophy should be are not constant, and so Socrates appears in a variety of roles. In the dialogues in which Socrates is marginal, Plato's conception of the philosopher goes beyond what he thinks Socrates can plausibly represent. And where Socrates is the main figure it is wiser to think of Plato as developing different aspects of what Socrates represents for him than to ask how close he is to (or far from) the "real" Socrates.

· · · · ·

Socrates thought of himself as seeking for the truth. He looked for it, however, in a radically new way. Refusing to produce grand theories of the world, or philosophical treatises—refusing, indeed, to write anything philosophical—he sought the truth by talking to individuals and pressing on them the importance of understanding what was being talked about. Plato was obviously impressed by

Socrates' insistence that the grander tasks of philosophy will have to wait until we achieve understanding of what we take for granted—courage, justice, and other virtues, the idea of living a good life, our own claims to understanding. Socrates identified the philosophical life as one of continuing inquiry and investigation, into others' beliefs and one's own. Plato was profoundly impressed by Socrates' insistence on putting inquiry before doctrine, and the search for understanding before ambitious claims. Socrates also took the philosophical life as one to be lived seriously, and died rather than compromise his values in defending his life. The best measure of Plato's respect for Socrates is the fact that in most of the dialogues he wrote Socrates is the main figure, and there is only one dialogue (the Laws) in which he does not appear at all. Rather than write in his own person, Plato chose always to present Socrates as the figure of the philosopher searching for truth.

At some point in his life, which we cannot pinpoint accurately, Plato made two momentous decisions. He rejected his family and civic duty of marrying and producing heirs. (Modern readers are unsurprised that Plato never married, because his writings seem so obviously homosexual in temperament. But in ancient Athens marriage was a duty for the continuance of the family and the city, and had nothing to do with personal sexuality. In not marrying, Plato was giving up having posterity of his own, a great loss in his society.) And he founded the first school of philosophy, called the Academy after the gymnasium where it met.

Plato made two critical decisions at some point in his life. First, he decided to forgo marriage and a family, a dramatic choice in Athenian society at the time because he would be left with no heirs. Second, he founded the Academy, the first school of philosophy, and though this painting portrays Plato as a teacher in the Academy he founded, we know very little about the school's organization.

Greek philosopher Aristotle (384–322 BCE) was a student of Plato's, and although he disagreed fundamentally with some of Plato's ideas, he remained at the Academy for twenty years. This marble bust of Aristotle is a Roman copy after a Greek bronze original by Lysippos from 330 BCE; the alabaster mantle is a modern addition.

We know very little about the organization of the Academy, and academics of every generation have been tempted to see in it some of the structure of their own university system. Aristotle was there for twenty years, and when we hear of him teaching we are tempted to think of him as an advanced graduate student or junior professor; but we should remember that the Academy was always a public gymnasium, and that it is unlikely that Plato's school had many of the institutional features of a modern university. Plato did not charge fees, but only those wealthy enough to spend time on philosophy were able to attend for long. We know of one public lecture Plato gave, on "The Good," which was a fiasco because the audience came to hear about the good life, while Plato talked about mathematics. We have a parody of students in the Academy defining a vegetable. Otherwise, the picture we get of the Academy is of a center for discussions, with no indication that students went there to learn Platonic doctrines. Indeed, perhaps "students" is a misnomer; the first center of further education was in a world without degrees, grades, credentials, or tenure.

It is easy to see the founding of a philosophical school as being in tension with Plato's devotion to the memory of Socrates. Socrates, after all, rejected everything in philosophy that could be thought of as academic. Yet as Plato presents Socrates, seeking the truth through inquiry does not, as we shall see, preclude having positive opinions of your own. And the Academy was not a place where those who came had to learn to agree with Plato. Not only Plato's greatest pupil, Aristotle, but the next two heads of the Academy disagreed quite fundamentally with some of Plato's ideas. So the Academy can be seen as a school for learning to think philosophically, and so to continue in the tradition of Socrates.

In one respect, however, Plato can be said to have moved on quite decisively from Socrates, who lost interest in the theories of his time about the nature of the world and focused on questions of how to live. In the ancient world Plato was thought of as the first systematic philosopher, the first to see philosophy as a distinctive approach to what were later to be called logic, physics, and ethics. If we look at the dialogues as a whole, we can indeed see a large and systematic set of concerns—systematic in that they are a continuing set of concerns, though not a set of organized dogmas.

Both in antiquity and later, some have further systematized Plato's ideas as a set of doctrines, generally referred to as "Platonism," but this is a step Plato himself never takes. He leaves us with the dialogues, and we have to do for ourselves the work of extracting and organizing his thoughts.

Plato is the first thinker to demarcate philosophy as a subject and method in its own right, distinct from other approaches such as rhetoric and poetry. He is sometimes said to have been the inventor of philosophy because of this insistence on its difference from other forms of thought, and he seems to have been the first to use the word

In one sense, the founding of a philosophical school could be seen as in being in tension with Plato's devotion to the memory of Socrates, since Socrates eschewed all things academic in philosophy. This image from 1874 shows Plato meditating at the grave of Socrates.

philosophia, "love of wisdom," to capture what he has in mind. He is certainly the inventor of philosophy as a subject, as a distinctive way of thinking about, and relating to, a wide range of issues and problems. Philosophy in this sense is still taught and learned in schools and universities today.

THREE

Drama, Fiction, and
the Elusive Author

●

Theory and Practice

Plato goes out of his way many times to insist that philosophy is the search for truth, using methods of argument. At different times he puts forward different candidates for the best philosophical method, which he often calls "dialectic," but he never compromises on the point that philosophy has a different (and higher) aim, and a more austere method, than what he sees as its main cultural competitors. There has always been hostility, he says at

Plato abuses cultural forms that use persuasion to attract the audience to a conclusion rather than relying the intellectual force of the argument alone. Among the targets of his criticism was publicly performed dramatic and epic poetry, an example of which is shown in this hand-colored engraving of a performance at the Theater of Dionysus in ancient Athens from the 1891 German encyclopedia *Pierers Konversationslexikon*, edited by Joseph Kürschner.

the end of the *Republic*, between philosophy and poetry (he means publicly performed dramatic and epic poetry, not the private reading of short poems). And in the *Gorgias* and *Phaedrus* he establishes, in different ways, strong opposition between philosophy and the practice of rhetoric. Philosophy aims only at the truth, not at mere persuasion regardless of truth, which is a dubious enterprise in both its intentions and its methods. (Recall the jury's problem in Chapter 1.) Perhaps Plato is not so much building on already recognized distinctions between philosophy and other kinds of intellectual activity, as actually establishing them, by his pioneering of the idea that philosophy has its own aims and methods, that it forms a distinct, and distinctive, subject which we should demarcate from other ways of thinking. In any case, few philosophers have stressed as much as Plato the need to distinguish philosophy's procedures sharply from procedures that produce agreement by persuasive, nonrigorous means.

And yet Plato is the most "literary" philosopher, the philosopher most accessible to nonspecialists because of the readability and charm of (at least some of) his writings. Some of his works are as famous for their literary as for their philosophical aspects. Even the more subdued contain metaphors, comic passages, and other attention grabbers.

One of the most striking things about his works, moreover, is that they are all cast in a dramatic form—either a dialogue between two or more people or a monologue, sometimes reporting others' dialogue. Many of these writings characterize various speakers, guide the discussion, and keep the reader involved with great skill. Nothing could seem further from the specialized, often technical, and academic form in which most philosophers have written. Moreover, such "literary" devices seem obviously open to the objections Plato brings against the purveyors of mere persuasion: they attract the reader to the conclusions, rather than relying on the bare intellectual force of argument. How can so literary a writer be against what literature does? Is he not undermining what he himself is doing?

· · · · ·

SOCRATIC "IRONY"

Socrates is talking to Hippias of Elis, a traveling "sophist" who sets up as a professional "wise man," taking money for lessons in private and public rhetoric, and managing public business himself. How, Socrates asks, does Hippias explain the fact that wise men in the old days were not rich public figures?

HIPPIAS: What do you think it could be, Socrates, other than that they were incompetent and not capable of using their wisdom to achieve in both areas, public and private?

SOCRATES: Well, other skills have certainly improved, and by comparison with modern craftsmen the older ones are worthless. Are we to say that your skill—sophistry—has improved in the same way, and that the ancients who practiced wisdom were worthless compared to you?

HIPPIAS: Yes—you're completely right! . . .

SOCRATES: . . . None of those early thinkers thought it right to demand money as payment, or to make displays of their own wisdom before all sorts of people. That's how simpleminded they were; they didn't notice how valuable money is. But each of the modern people you mention [Gorgias and Prodicus] has made more money from his wisdom than any other craftsman from any skill. And Protagoras did it even before they did.

HIPPIAS: Socrates, you have no idea just how fine this is. If you knew how much money *I've* made, you'd be amazed! . . . I'm pretty sure that I've made more money than any two sophists you like put together!

SOCRATES: What a fine thing to say, Hippias! It's very indicative of your own wisdom, and of what a difference there is between people nowadays and the ancients.

(Hippias Major 281d–283b)

Hippias thinks Socrates is complimenting him. The reader, however, sees clearly that Socrates despises the use of intellect to make money, rather than to search for the truth, and hence has complete contempt for Hippias. Socrates is often "ironical" in this way, operating at the level of his interlocutor in such a way that the reader can see that he does not share it. This is not always an attractive trait, but it makes for many vivid and comic passages in Plato's writing.

PLATO'S WORKS

Unusually for an ancient philosopher, we can be fairly confident that we have all Plato's "published" works, including one unfinished fragment (*Critias*) and some short works which were attributed to Plato after his death but contain later style and vocabulary (these are marked by *). Works about which there is less consensus, which may be by Plato, are marked by †.

We have no external indications of the order in which Plato wrote his dialogues (except that the *Laws* seems to have been unfinished

Although we can be fairly certain that we have all of Plato's "published" works, there is no record of the order in which they were written, and there appears to have been no established order in which the works were discussed or taught in the ancient world. Many modern-day collections follow an organization created by the Platonist philosopher Thrasyllus for the works of the ancient Greek philosopher, who is shown here in an illustration from the *Nuremberg Chronicle*.

at his death). In the ancient world there was no one privileged order either for teaching the dialogues or for regarding them as a presentation of "Plato's philosophy"; much depended on the reader's interests, aptitude, and level of philosophical sophistication.

The following order of the dialogues was established by Thrasyllus, a Platonist philosopher who was also the Emperor Tiberius's private astrologer. Thrasyllus put the dialogues in groups of four for reasons which are not always clear. His order has been used by many editions of Plato's text, as well as by the Hackett translation of the complete works of Plato.

Euthyphro, Apology (Socrates' Defense), Crito, Phaedo, Cratylus, Theaetetus, Sophist, Statesman, Parmenides, Philebus, Symposium, Phaedrus, Alcibiades, Second Alcibiades*, Hipparchus, Lovers†, Theages†, Charmides, Laches, Lysis, Euthydemus, Protagoras, Gorgias, Meno, Greater Hippias, Lesser Hippias, Ion, Menexenus, Clitophon, Republic, Timaeus, Critias, Minos*, Laws, Epinomis*, Letters†, Definitions*, On Justice*, On Virtue*, Demodocus*, Sisyphus*, Halycon*, Eryxias*, Axiochus*, Epigrams†

· · · · ·

Detachment and Authority

We can answer this by the thought that Plato is, indeed, undermining his own philosophical activity, systematically denouncing the form he uses. We can take him to be doing this either naively, simply not noticing that he uses persuasive techniques to abuse persuasion, or else with a sophisticated theory in mind of upsetting the reader's expectations. But there is a simpler, less extreme explanation which fits much better with the content of Plato's views on knowledge.

In presenting his works in the form of dialogue (direct or reported), Plato is detaching himself, as the possessor of philosophical views, from the views of the characters. The author is obviously present in all the characters in the dialogue, since Plato is writing all the parts. The reader is presented with the development of a debate between two or more people, and so with an argument, but then it is up to her to make what she can of it; the author does not present her with conclusions to be accepted on grounds that have the author's authority.

This point has sometimes been ignored, by interpreters who abstract Plato's ideas from the dialogue form and treat them as though they were written out in treatise form. And it has sometimes been exaggerated, by interpreters who refuse to move from the dialogue to ascribing any positive ideas to Plato at all. So it is worth examining first what does *not* follow from recognizing that Plato detaches himself from the characters' views in all his works by writing in dramatic form.

It doesn't follow that Plato is detached in the way that the author of an actual play is; he is not constructing a dramatic world in which the figures interact for our entertainment. Plato's works raise serious issues for the reader to engage with; they are meant to get the reader involved in doing philosophy, not just enjoying the drama. Hence, Plato doesn't present all the characters as equally deserving of our time and attention. Some are obnoxious or ridiculous, and others are colorless. The main character in many dialogues is Socrates, and it is obvious that he is often idealized, and put forward as the embodiment of philosophical activity in contrast to other kinds of life (what this is differs between different dialogues).

Plato's use of the dialogue form is perfectly consistent with his having a position on the issues discussed, and with his sometimes ascribing that position to Socrates. In some dialogues Socrates argues with another person, showing him that he lacks understanding of some matter on which he thought he was an expert, but Socrates himself puts forward no positive views on the issue, and may even declare that he also lacks understanding. It does not at all follow that Plato has no position on the matter. Plato uses the character Socrates in many ways, not simply to put forward his own views.

Why does Plato distance himself in this way? If he does have positions, and if it is clear enough to the reader that if anybody in the dialogues presents these views it will be Socrates, then what is the point of writing in a dramatic form? Why doesn't Plato just come out and tell us what his position is?

Plato very much wants not to present his own position for the reader to accept on Plato's authority. He was aware of philosophers who wrote authoritative treatises, telling their readers what to think about a number of large and important matters. Plato has very substantial and strongly held views on a number of issues; that is why he is so prominent in Western philosophy. But he also sees himself as a follower of Socrates, who wrote nothing, but examined the views of others, trying to get them to understand for themselves. Plato wants the reader to come to understand what is said for himself or herself. As we shall see in more detail when we consider his views on knowledge and understanding (and as we have already had a glimpse in the jury passage—recall

Chapter 1), the reader is made to do his or her own work to come to understand what Plato is saying. Plato is sure that he is right on a number of issues, but he doesn't want the reader to pick up these views just because Plato says so.

It is easy to miss this point, because in some of Plato's most famous dialogues Socrates is made to expound positive positions confidently and at some length, while the people he is talking to (the "interlocutors") are given only comments like, "Quite true, Socrates." We may think that in these passages there is no real distancing; what Socrates says is just what Plato thinks. But Plato cannot know anything for you; you have to do your own work to achieve understanding of what is going on. Sometimes, indeed, the reader is aided in this by finding that Socrates' claims are contested, or that he is on the defensive, or that the overall intention of a passage, or a dialogue, is obscure. Further, formal detachment of Plato from what is being said by Socrates (or, in some works, by a Visitor from Elea) is always important, even where it is not dramatically very lively. For, even if you have worked out what Plato thinks, there is still work to do; it isn't *your* thought, as opposed to Plato's, until you have thought it through for yourself, rather than just passively taking it in as being what Plato says. Only then can it become something you understand.

In one famous passage, Plato shows us Socrates comparing himself to a midwife, who delivers other people's ideas and tests them, rather than having "children" of his own. The metaphor doesn't imply that Socrates has no ideas of his own; it implies that he keeps two things separate: having his own ideas, and testing the ideas of others. Plato writes philosophy as he does because he is concerned to keep two things apart also: presenting his own positions, and getting the reader to come to understand them for herself. Few philosophers have presented their ideas as passionately as Plato. But he never confuses this with foisting his ideas on the reader; formally, the reader never faces Plato's own ideas, only ideas he presents in a detached way through other people.

· · · · ·

SOCRATES THE MIDWIFE

Socrates, the son of a midwife, Phaenarete, claims to practice a kind of midwifery himself.

This at least is true of me as well as of midwives: I am barren of wisdom, and it's a true reproach that many people have made about me, that I ask other people questions but never put forward my own position about anything, because I don't have anything wise to say. This is the reason for it: the god compels me to be a midwife, but has forbidden me to give birth. So I myself am hardly a wise person, and I have no such discovery either that has been born as the offspring of my soul. Take people who associate with me, however. At first some of them seem quite stupid, but as the association goes on all those to whom the god grants it turn out to make amazing progress, as others think as well as themselves. But this is clear: they have never learned anything from me; rather they have discovered within themselves many fine things, and brought them to birth. And for the delivery the god and I myself are responsible.

(Theaetetus 150c–d)

Some think, on the basis of passages like these, that Plato is an Academic, having no beliefs.

Why *did* god tell Socrates, in the *Theaetetus*, to be a midwife to others, but not to give birth himself? . . . Suppose that nothing can be apprehended and known by humans: then it was reasonable for god to prevent Socrates giving birth to bogus beliefs, false and baseless, and to force him to test others who had opinions of that kind. Argument that rids you of the greatest evil—deception and pretentiousness—is no small help, rather a major one. . . . This was Socrates, healing, not of the body but of the festering and corrupted soul. But suppose

there *is* knowledge of the truth, and that there is one truth—then this is had not just by the person who discovers it but no less by the person who learns from the discoverer. But you are more likely to get it if you are not already convinced that you have it, and then you get the best of all, just as you can adopt an excellent child without having given birth yourself.

Greek biographer and moralist Plutarch (ca. 46 CE–after 119) is shown in this French line engraving from 1541.

(Plutarch, Platonic Question 1)

Two Traditions

In the ancient world there were two traditions of reading Plato, and of identifying yourself as one of his philosophical followers. The less familiar to us came first. After a period following Plato's death when his successors in the Academy developed their own ideas about metaphysics and morality, the Academy was (around 268 BCE) recalled by a new head, Arcesilaus, to the method of argument exemplified in the dialogues in which Socrates is shown arguing with someone but not positively stating or arguing for his own position. Arcesilaus identified this feature of Socratic argument—arguing with the other person *on his own terms*, showing him that *he* has a problem regardless of what you think—as the most important aspect of doing philosophy in Plato's way. He probably appealed to Plato's use of dialogue to detach himself from the positions put forward in order to hold that the positive claims we find in Plato, however confidently stated, always have the status merely of positions put forward for discussion, even where it is relatively clear that Plato thinks them correct. At any rate, he put Plato's school on a course which is, in ancient terms, "skeptical"—that is, inquiring and questioning the credentials of others' views, rather than committed to particular philosophical beliefs of one's own. This "New" or Skeptical Academy continued as Plato's school, teaching people to argue against current dogmas, until the institution came to an end in the first century BCE.

Not until Plato's own school had ended do we find a tradition starting, called "Platonist" as opposed to the inquiring "Academy," in which interpreters think of Plato's works as putting forward a system of ideas, taken to be "Platonism." For this tradition, it is Plato's positive claims that are interesting, not just his insistence on argument to demolish the claims of others and to enable one's own understanding

Plato's Academy continued to operate after his death, and around 268 BCE, its head at the time, Arcesilaus, had the school return to its former method of argument, in which the philosopher espouses no point of his own but argues with another person on his or her own terms, thus beginning the so-called Skeptical School. The remains of the Academy, shown here in a recent photograph, are believed to have been found in the Akadimia Platonos subdivision of Athens, Greece.

of others' positions. From the first century BCE to the end of antiquity we find philosophers producing commentaries on Plato's dialogues, designed to help readers with the language, the details, and the arguments. They also wrote introductions to Plato, in which Plato's thought is set out as a philosophical system, often in the later ancient format of three parts: logic (and epistemology), physics (and metaphysics), and ethics (and politics). When Plato's thought is treated in this way, the dialogues are thought of as sources for his position on various issues.

This second tradition has been divided by modern interpreters into the "Middle Platonists," who produced on the whole dutiful and academic but unexciting work, and "Neo-Platonists," who, beginning from Plotinus's brilliant rethinking of Plato in the third century CE, developed Plato's thought in original and innovative ways. But this is a modern distinction; in the ancient world the only real distinction was seen as that between two traditions. On the one hand, there was the "skeptical," inquiring Academy tradition of taking from Plato the practice of arguing on the opponent's terms and detaching yourself from commitment to your conclusions as authoritative pronouncements. On the other, there was the Platonist tradition, "doctrinal" or "dogmatic," for which what mattered were Plato's actual ideas

Egyptian-born Roman philosopher Plotinus (205–270 CE), shown here in an illustration from the *Nuremberg Chronicle*, is credited with the founding of Neoplatonism, a school of thought that developed Plato's philosophy in original and innovative ways.

about the soul, the cosmos, virtue, and happiness. For thinkers in this second tradition, philosophical activity took the form of lovingly studying Plato's works, developing his ideas further in contemporary terms, or both.

It is the "dogmatic" Platonist tradition which is most familiar to us. We find it natural for there to be editions and translations of Plato's texts, commentaries on them, and both scholarly and popular books about his ideas (such as this one, of course), even if we are less likely to expect modern philosophers to develop Platonic themes. The alternative tradition, that it is Plato's method of doing philosophy that he wants us to engage with rather than his own ideas, has been present only fitfully in the twentieth century, and has usually taken eccentric forms that have prevented its being taken seriously. It has become better known in the last few years, as students of ancient philosophy have taken more interest in ancient methods of arguing.

Do these traditions have to be mutually hostile? At times they have been; but it is possible for them to coexist and even learn from each other. Even if you think that what is interesting about Plato is his ideas about the soul, Forms, or the good life, you can learn a lot from the way Plato distances himself from commitment and stresses the importance of arguing on the opponent's terms. And even if you think that what is compelling in Plato is his picture of Socrates, always inquiring and never claiming knowledge, it is interesting to work out the positive views within which Plato has Socrates function in this way.

PLATO THE SKEPTIC?

Is Plato a skeptic—that is, in ancient terms, does he identify philosophical activity with questioning the claims of others, rather than putting forward conclusions as justified?

Cicero puts the case for saying yes:

The skeptical Academy is called the New Academy, but it seems to me we can also call it the Old Academy, if we ascribe Plato to the New as well as the Old Academy. In his works nothing is stated firmly, and there are many arguments on both sides of a question. Everything is subject to inquiry, and nothing is stated as certain.

This bust of Roman statesman, orator, and author Marcus Tullius Cicero (106–43 BCE) was created by Danish/Icelandic sculptor Bertel Thorvaldsen in 1799 or 1800.

Sextus Empiricus, a different kind of skeptic, says no:

As for Plato, some have said that he is dogmatic, others aporetic, others partly aporetic and partly dogmatic (for in the gymnastic works, where Socrates is introduced either as playing with people or as contesting with sophists, they say that his distinctive character is gymnastic and aporetic; but that he is dogmatic where he makes

Greek physician and philosopher Sextus Empiricus (ca. 160–ca. 210 CE) is shown here in a 1692 copper engraving after an ancient coin.

assertions seriously through Socrates or Timaeus or someone similar. . . .) Here . . . we say . . . that when Plato makes assertions about Forms or about the existence of Providence or about a virtuous life being preferable to a life of vice, then if he assents to these things as being really so, he is holding beliefs; and if he commits himself to them as being more plausible, he has abandoned the distinctive character of Skepticism. . . .

• • • • •

Many Voices?

"Plato has many voices, not, as some think, many doctrines." So says Arius Didymus, an ancient scholarly philosopher, aware that when we read the dialogues, we become progressively more puzzled as to how they are supposed to add up. Even if we assume that the positions defended in some dialogues by Socrates, or the Visitor from Elea, are all at least provisionally accepted by Plato, we find differences of emphasis and perspective which make it difficult to judge how important a given theme is, as well as radically different treatments of similar ideas and sometimes what look like outright conflicts between the positions in different dialogues.

Over the centuries there have been many reactions to this. One is to hold that Plato wrote his dialogues to be read separately, and that it is mistaken to try to build up a system of ideas from them jointly. It is hard to refute this position, but it is also revealingly hard to carry it through, to read *Apology*, *Crito*, and *Gorgias*, for example, as though the claims about goodness and happiness in them were quite unconnected. And when we read what is said about pleasure in the *Protagoras* and then go on to find an apparently conflicting position in the *Gorgias*, it is unsatisfactory just to reflect that these are different dialogues. There are strands of thought which run through many of Plato's dialogues, and encourage us to try to put the ideas together.

What kind of unity do we find in these ideas, however? Some interpreters find a very high degree of unity, but at the cost of dismissing, or downgrading, what look like different approaches in different dialogues. The ancient Platonists tend to do this. The extreme version of this view sees "Platonism" as a monolithic set of ideas in Plato's mind independent of his presentation of them in the dialogues, and also independent

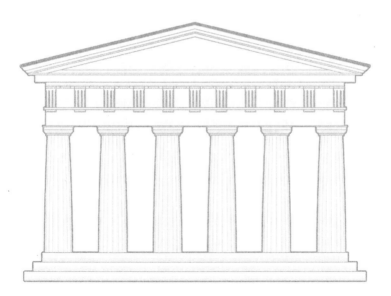

of his development of arguments for them. Proponents of this view have given Plato a bad name among philosophers, as being more interested in dogma than in argument. In the twentieth century more attention has been paid to the details of Plato's arguments, and interpreters have been more open to the thought that he may have returned to the same idea more than once, not always in the same way. Until recently it was a standard assumption of Plato scholarship that Plato's works display a "development" of his thought, from early dialogues which represent Socrates as arguing without coming to conclusions, to the "middle" and "late" dialogues in which Plato puts forward his own ideas. The developmental view rests on questionable assumptions about Plato's life, about the possibility of dating texts, and about reading Socrates as simply a mouthpiece for Plato, and is nowadays much queried. It does have answers for some problems created by apparently conflicting passages, but there are other ways of meeting these problems.

Plato's ideas can be seen as hanging together tightly or loosely. They can also be seen as more or less dogmatically put forward. Many doctrinal Platonists have been insensitive to Plato's refusal to commit himself in person; they too have given Plato a bad name among philosophers, as though he were simply using Socrates, or the Eleatic Visitor, as a mouthpiece to pontificate. But we can respect Plato's refusal to dogmatize while remaining interested in his ideas. Many people find that as they read through the dialogues they get an increasingly cumulative impression of a distinctive set of ideas; they can also recognize that Plato's statements of these ideas is never more than provisional.

Fiction, Myth, and Philosophy

The philosopher aims at truth—and so should have no use for the kind of enterprise we call fiction, where we entertain ourselves by stories we know are not true. Plato goes further, and is notoriously hostile to the fictions popular in his culture, mainly taking the form of publicly performed drama and recitation. He is aware of the power that such narratives have to shape our conceptions of ourselves and of the social world we live in. He is strongly against such power when used thoughtlessly to propagate traditional ideas, which can be harmful. In the *Republic* especially, Plato makes the case that the traditional cultural education of his time leaves people with false beliefs about the gods and false ideals to live up to. The stories found in Homer and the ancient dramatists (which played the role taken in our society by popular entertainment) glamorize the values of a warrior society, and are bound to unfit people for living in civic society, where they must act in cooperation with others.

This Hellenistic terra cotta figurine (second century BCE), shows an actor wearing the mask of a rustic.

Especially in the *Republic*, a fragment of which is shown here on a papyrus from Oxyrhynchus, Egypt, Plato condemned the traditional cultural education of his time as leaving people with false beliefs and false ideals to live up to.

Plato is intensely hostile to the way that what we would call creativity and imagination are thoughtlessly put to trivial or damaging ends. But he is, as already noted, a creative and imaginative writer himself, and hardly unaware of this. His commitment to the philosophical search for truth alters his attitude to his own gifts in two ways.

Firstly, he thinks of their role as limited. Some of the dialogues are written in ways that will draw in the unphilosophical, but this is a level at which we are not encouraged to stay. Even in the easier, attractive dialogues there is always a clear message that philosophy goes on to

According to Plato, the work of Greek epic poet Homer (ninth–ca. eighth century BCE) and other ancient dramatists, which glamorized the warrior society, were bound to make people unfit for living in a civilized society. Homer is shown here in a 1663 oil-on-canvas portrait by Rembrandt.

argue, to examine, and to test claims in a way that leaves behind their appeal to the imagination.

And further, Plato rejects the idea that imagination and creativity have value of their own; he uses them only in the service of furthering what he takes to be true positions. One of his most notorious views, one that has recommended him to puritans in every age, is his rejection of

the idea of harmless entertainment. For him the appeal of a good story is valuable if it encourages us to think of, and think further about, good values; otherwise it is harmful, since it encourages us to feel satisfied with the unquestioned values of our culture.

Hence Plato is quite ready, in his own writings, to use traditional forms such as narrative, descriptive images, and myth, stories involving the superhuman. Their content, though, is thoroughly transformed, particularly with respect to myth, where Plato rejects his culture's acceptance of a plurality of mutually indifferent or hostile gods interfering in human life, replacing it by a form of monotheism in which god is responsible only for what is good. Plato's elaborate myths, in the *Gorgias*, *Phaedo*, *Republic*, *Phaedrus*, and *Statesman*, underline the points made through argument in the dialogue by using them as materials for an imaginative narrative.

One irony here is that in terms of sheer numbers of people affected, probably the most influential thing Plato ever wrote was his unfinished story of Atlantis, in the introduction to *Timaeus* and the fragment *Critias*. He begins a narrative about ancient Athens, which embodied an ideal form of government, and a threatened invasion by Atlantis, a rich, sophisticated civilization to the west of the known Greek world. Atlantis itself was originally Utopian also, but it is flawed, in ways that lead it to seek imperialist conquest. Even the beginnings of this story have inspired a

Despite its intended purpose—to get the reader to examine the ideas of government and power— Plato's unfinished fictional story of Atlantis, which appears in *Timaeus* and the fragment *Critias*, has instead appealed to people who are determined to undercover a previously hidden version of history. As a result, the "real" Atlantis has been found in locations throughout the world. This idealistic 1928 illustration by J. Augustus Knapp, from *The Secret Teachings of All Ages: An Encyclopedic Outline of Masonic, Hermetic, Qabbalistic and Rosicrucian Symbolical Philosophy*, by Manly P. Hall, depicts the Atlantean Mystery Temple.

genre of Utopian writing, as well as romances, action stories, and movies about exotic outsiders threatening "our" civilization. (Most of these are cruder than Plato's, which offers its readers no easy identification with "the good guys," and no straightforwardly optimistic ending.)

Most interesting, however, is that Plato has his narrator begin the story with a long preamble about getting it from Egyptian priests, who have, he says, far older records than the Greeks, whose civilization has frequently been destroyed and risen again, so that they are ignorant of their own history. This idea has a deep appeal for many people determined to uncover a hitherto hidden version of "our history." The "real" Atlantis has been "discovered" in the Mediterranean, on the island of Thera and at the site of Troy, and west of the Mediterranean, in prehistoric Britain, Ireland, Denmark, South America, the Yucatán, the Bahamas, North America, and as a lost continent now sunk in the Atlantic.

The continuing industry of discovering Atlantis illustrates the dangers of reading Plato. For he is clearly using what has become a standard device of fiction—stressing the historicity of an event (and the discovery of hitherto unknown authorities) as an indication that what follows is fiction. The idea is that we should use the story to examine our ideas of government and power. We have missed the point if instead of thinking about these issues we go off exploring the seabed. The continuing misunderstanding of Plato as historian here enables us to see why his distrust of imaginative writing is sometimes justified.

FOUR

Love, Sex, Gender, and Philosophy

●

Not Seeing Plato Whole

Plato is, according to Saint Augustine, the pagan philosopher who comes nearest to Christianity. In their eagerness to co-opt Plato's authority in the intellectual development of the church, however, Augustine and other church fathers looked away from something in Plato which was anathema to Judaism and Christianity, and thus began an unfortunate tradition of selective and sometimes dishonest attention to Plato's works.

Plato wrote in a society in which sexual and erotic relations between men were taken for granted, and were often socially acceptable, particularly between an adolescent boy and an adult man, where the older "lover" served

This detail from the tondo of a red-figure Attic cup, ca. 480 BCE, by the so-called Briseis Painter, depicts one aspect of the socially acceptable sexual and erotic relations between men in ancient Greek society, an adult man, the "lover," and an adolescent boy, his "beloved," sharing a kiss.

as the younger "beloved's" mentor and guide to the adult world. Such relationships were romanticized, and not regarded as competitors to more prosaic relationships like marriage.

Plato's treatment of love as background to and possibly part of philosophy is mostly to be found in the dialogues *Symposium* and *Phaedrus*, although it forms part of the setting of some other dialogues. In what follows (and for the rest of the book), I shall talk of Plato's views, assuming that the reader will not need constant repetition of the points we have noted about the distancing produced by the dialogue form.

Plato goes beyond accepting homoerotic relationships as part of his social world. He takes the romantic view of them, and takes it further, in two ways. He stresses the mentoring aspect of the lover-beloved relation, elevating it to an idealized relation between teacher and pupil which is above physical attraction and consists in concern for the other's soul—that is, their psychological and mental well-being. This is what is often labeled "Platonic love"— love with the form of a romantic relation, but transformed by concern with the soul rather than the body. Socrates is often depicted as concerned with the well-being of young boys with whom he hangs out at the gymnasia. Indeed, sometimes he claims to be an expert on love (*ta erotika*, love of the sexual and romantic sort).

This is, of course, liable to misunderstanding. Older men who hang round gymnasia are usually, after all, interested in young men's bodies, not their souls. In the *Symposium* there is a passage (215a–222b) designed to show what Socrates' love really is. Alcibiades, a beautiful, brilliant, and rich young Athenian, is used to being pursued by older men, and becomes fascinated by the way Socrates refuses to be drawn by his glamour. He discovers that only Socrates is capable of getting him to feel ashamed of his superficial way of life and to aspire to be

In Plato's *Symposium*, one character is the beautiful, brilliant, and rich young Athenian Alcibiades, shown here in a marble bust, a Roman copy after a Greek original of the fourth century BCE. The young Athenian, used to the attentions of older men but fascinated by Socrates' refusal to be drawn to his glamour, finds that only Socrates can make him feel ashamed of his superficial life and inspire him to try to become a better person.

a better person. Wanting Socrates as his mentor, he resolves to seduce him into a sexual relationship. But, humiliatingly, he fails, even when he moves from flirtation to spending the night with Socrates under the same cloak. Socrates merely comments that, if he could indeed make Alcibiades a better person, this would be a prize worth a great deal more than mere sex.

Despite the eloquence of this passage, misunderstanding was not always averted. The later satirist Lucian has a Platonist philosopher reassure a father nervous about having him as a tutor for his teenage son: it is the soul that interests him, he says, not the body, and even when his pupils spend the night under the same cloak—they never complain!

Love and Sex

Indeed, some passages, particularly in the *Phaedrus*, suggest that sex is not totally excluded from a continuing philosophical relationship (not, however, the highest sort), once it has progressed beyond the mentor-pupil relationship to one of a more equal philosophical companionship. For Plato sex as such is not the problem here; the issue is the extent to which lives can be dedicated to the study of philosophy without becoming indifferent to the demands of everyday life.

There is a second way in which Plato uses the language of homo-erotic romantic love. Most notably in the *Symposium*, he represents the urge to philosophical inquiry and understanding as itself being a transformation of sexual desire. In a passage on the "ascent of love," Socrates describes how erotic urging can become sublimated and transfigured, leading the person to move beyond particular gratifica-tions, finding satisfaction only in the transformation from individual

In his *Symposium*, Plato suggests that the urge to philosophical inquiry is a transformation of sexual desire. The 1873 oil on canvas *Plato's Symposium* is Anselm Feuerbach's interpretation of Plato's philosophical gathering, in which the guests give speeches in honor of love.

possession to contemplation and understanding universal truths. Plato's ideas here have been compared to Freud's, though they are arguably less reductive: the human urge to understand is traced to a basic drive we all share, but one which can, while retaining its energy and urgency, be transformed into something with intellectual structure and complexity.

Why does Plato do anything as unlikely as trace the drive for philosophical understanding to the energy of love? Perhaps because he is attracted, as often, by an explanation which has the promise of harmonizing two very different demands on what is to be explained. The drive to do philosophy has to come from within you, and be genuine. Plato is struck by its likeness to the lover's desire: it comes from within you in a way that cannot be deliberately produced, and, like love, it drives you to focus all your efforts to achieve an aim which you feel you cannot live without, however impossible attainment may seem. But philosophy is also a joint activity; and few have stressed as much as Plato the importance of mutual discussion and argument; philosophical achievement is produced from the conversations of two or more, not just the intense thoughts of one. Plato stresses at times the way that love can produce a couple with joint concerns which transcend what each gets separately out of the relationship; philosophy similarly requires the stimulus and cooperation of joint discussion and argument. Philosophy and love thus share puzzling features. How far love illuminates philosophy is another matter; certainly Plato's discussion locates the place of both in human life in a way that is original and inspiring.

Gender Trouble

Inspiring to men, perhaps. But isn't there a problem for women reading these works, in which romantic and erotic love is discussed entirely in homoerotic terms, and women are not considered, or brought in only as an inferior or rejected option? Plato talks of love between men producing intellectual "offspring" which are far to be preferred to the mere physical offspring that men and women produce together. Here he is probably just picking up contemporary contempt for the feminine sphere in taking love between men to be superior, intellectually and otherwise, to heterosexual love; though he probably exaggerates this contempt, as well as the significance of homoerotic love in his society. (Love between women does not interest him much; probably he knew little about it.) However, Plato's attitude to women is complex. He is obviously not concerned about women's sensitivities in his writings. But in the *Symposium* the account of the "ascent" of love is actually put into the mouth of a woman, a priestess called Diotima. And alongside the misogyny, Plato perceives that there is a problem about women's lives and their expectations, a problem philosophers have until recently rarely appreciated.

Women's Potential, and the Family

Plato's *Republic*, and to a lesser extent *Laws*, are famous for the idea that in an ideally governed society the nuclear family would be either abolished or severely limited. Plato is struck by the way that families often serve as schools of selfishness and a competitive and hostile attitude to outsiders, and that this often closes off the spread of attachment to wider groups. Cities will have citizens with real attachment to their city and its ideals, he thinks, only if the kind of influences provided within the nuclear family are reined in. Among the benefits of this idea he sees a release of the potential in women, who will exchange a narrow life of caring for husband and children at home for

A Greek woman is depicted grinding wheat in this terra cotta figurine (ca. 450 BCE) from Kameiros, Rhodes, which is housed in the British Museum in London.

one in which their physical and mental capacities can be developed in wider contexts, just as those of men are.

In the *Republic* this idea is developed in a very idealized context in which it is assumed that women can become both warriors and philosophers in the way that men do. In the *Laws* the context is nearer to that of Plato's world, and women are allowed some expansion of role beyond traditional ones, though the nuclear family is retained. These ideas, even in a narrower version, were revolutionary in Plato's day, calling forth ridicule and misunderstanding.

In a period when the issues have been thoroughly debated in an organized way, we can clearly see many defects in Plato's approach. It is entirely unempirical, resting on a priori claims about human nature, and hence has no clear application to actual societies. As a heroic but unrealistic ideal, it has made little actual impact through the centuries. Further, despite being theoretically committed to equality between the sexes, Plato persists in thinking that women will on the whole perform at a lower standard than men, both physically and mentally. And there is a reason for this: he thinks of improving the lot of women by enabling them to do what men do, and to play the roles that men play. He sees nothing in women and their activities as they are in his society that is worthy of respect, or of retention as something that both men and women should do. This is a major reason why he continues to refer to women in misogynistic terms.

So we can see why some have thought of Plato as the first feminist, because he sees no reason why women should be barred from activities that men do, while others have seen in him a deeply antifeminist strain, holding that women are worth thinking about only to the extent that they can be socially reconstructed as men. Considering the difficulty of the issue, and the way that feminism tends to divide on the subject of whether traditionally feminine activities and traits should be rejected or valued, we can appreciate why Plato sends mixed messages here. It is open to us to attack him for his lack of appreciation for what women actually are and do. Or we can be impressed by the fact that Plato does in fact see that the position of women in society is a problem, and that ideally something would be done about it. It is one of the marks of his originality that almost no other philosophers have thought this. Aristotle, for example, with greater respect for existing views, finds no problem at all in the fact that women run domestic homes, lack political rights, and are not educated as men are; and until recently he has been typical.

There is a story that there were two women pupils in the Academy, Lastheneia, and Axiothea, who came to the school disguised as a man after reading the *Republic*. The story may be an invention in the light of the *Republic*, but, whether historically true or not, it illustrates the way in which Plato was seen as holding that gender is irrelevant to intellectual development.

Sex and Gender

Until the twentieth century, while Plato has often been prominent in the Western philosophical tradition, his views on sex, love, and gender have been, for different reasons, regarded as off-limits to philosophical discussion, and this has resulted in a curious willed blindness to what is in the texts. Though not invented then, the hypocrisy involved was particularly apparent in the nineteenth century, when Plato's works became prominent in university education.

• • • • •

VICTORIAN EVASION OF THE HOMOEROTIC ELEMENT IN PLATO

Tom Stoppard's play *The Invention of Love* captures the ambivalence of Victorian Oxford's attitude to Plato. Here we meet Walter Pater, a repressed homosexual whose book *Plato and Platonism* brought some aspects of Plato's love of male beauty almost to the surface, and Benjamin Jowett, the Master of Balliol College, who translated Plato into English and pioneered the study of Plato, particularly the *Republic*, at Oxford. In Stoppard's play Jowett charges Pater with writing inappropriately fervid letters to a Balliol student.

PATER: . . . I am astonished that you should take exception to an obviously Platonic enthusiasm.

John Wood and Ben Parker starred in Tom Stoppard's *The Invention of Love* (1997) at the Theatre Royal Haymarket (November 1998).

JOWETT: A Platonic enthusiasm as far as Plato was concerned meant an enthusiasm of the kind that would empty the public schools and fill the prisons where it is not nipped in the bud. In my translation of the Phaedrus it required all my ingenuity to rephrase his description of paederastia into the affectionate regard as exists between an Englishman and his wife. Plato would have made the transposition himself if he had had the good fortune to be a Balliol man.

PATER: And yet, Master, no amount of ingenuity can dispose of boy-love as the distinguishing feature of a society which we venerate as one of the most brilliant in the history of human culture, raised far above its neighbours in moral and mental distinction.

JOWETT: You are very kind but one undergraduate is hardly a distinguishing feature, and I have written to his father to remove him. . . . The canker that brought low the glory that was Greece shall not prevail over Balliol!

· · · · ·

Homosexuality was literally unspeakable, and Plato was made available in bowdlerized and misleading translations. At the same time, there was a general anxious half awareness that Platonic love was not socially approved heterosexual love.

The idea that men's social roles should be available to women, while not literally unspeakable, was regarded as a joke, until women's

FREE LOVE AND WOMEN'S RIGHTS.

LADY CUSTOMER—"Mr. Smith—ah, ah—have you any Her-books?"
BOOKSELLER—(Slightly surprised)—"Her-books, ma'am? I really——"
LADY CUSTOMER—"Ah, well, you naughty men call them Hymn-books. But, as we of the angelic sex are resolved on freeing ourselves from the chains imposed on us by tyrant man, we want Her-books in future!"
[Bookseller faints.]

Plato's idea that men's social roles should be available to women was regarded as revolutionary in his time, and considered a joke until more than two thousand years later. The caption to this late-nineteenth-century cartoon says, "Lady Customer— 'Mr. Smith—ah, ah—have you any Her-books?' Bookseller—(Slightly surprised)—'HER-books, ma'am? I really—' Lady Customer—'Ah, well, you naughty men call them Hymn-books. But, as we of the angelic sex are resolved on freeing ourselves from the chains imposed on us by tyrant man, we want Her-books in future.' [Bookseller faints.]"

By the time women's rights began to be taken seriously, Plato's work had little to add to the discussion, resting as it did on a priori claims about human nature. Among those at the forefront of the women's rights movement in the nineteenth century was Lucy Stone, who with social reformer Henry Blackwell founded the weekly newspaper the *Woman's Journal* in furtherance of the cause; the front page of the March 8, 1913, issue is shown here.

movements in the nineteenth century turned it into a serious subject of political discourse. For 150 years the *Republic* in particular has been discussed with this issue in mind. By this point, studying Plato has little to contribute to modern feminist discussion: his starting points and many of his assumptions are too remote from ours for him to be a profitable partner in debate for very long.

Yet it is in his attitude to women that Plato is most radical and pioneering. Even to have the idea that there is nothing natural about women's social roles, that they can do what men do, is a surprising breakthrough. However, original though his ideas about love and philosophy are, his focus on homoerotic love, when we look at it dispassionately, required much less originality. It has been the troubled attitude of so many later readers to this topic that has inflated it to the status of a major issue.

FIVE

Virtue, in Me and in My Society

●

How to Be Happy

In many dialogues Plato grapples with the question of how we are to live a good life. He begins from an assumption which he shares with the rest of his society, namely that we all seek happiness (*eudaimonia*). What we think of as ethics emerges as the concern not just to *live* one's life, but to do it *well*, to make a good job of it. We all seek to be happy, in the sense of living a good life (something to be sharply distinguished from modern notions of happiness, which identify it with feeling good; happiness in all ancient thinkers is the achievement of someone who lives an admirable, enviable life). Plato never doubts that this is where ethical concern starts. He gives, however, a radically

---

According to Plato, to lead a happy life, you must lead a virtuous life. Andrea Andreani's allegorical chiaroscuro woodcut *Virtue Chained by Love, Error, Ignorance, and Opinion* is from 1585.

different answer than most people, and most other philosophers, to the question of what it is to live an admirable, enviable life, and so to achieve happiness.

Many people, in the modern as much as in the ancient world, find it natural to say that a happy life is one in which you are successful; the happy person will be, typically, the rich, secure person who has achieved something in life. It sounds odd, indeed perverse, to say that someone could be happy, could be living a life you admire and try to emulate, if he or she turned out to be rejected and unsuccessful. But Plato was influenced by the example of Socrates, who gave up worldly success for philosophy, and who ended up condemned as a criminal and executed—yet who clearly seemed to Plato to have lived an admirable life. And so, most people must be wrong about how to achieve a happy life.

Where do most people go wrong? They think that their life will go well, and that they will be happy, if they have the things that most people think are good—health, wealth, good looks, and so on. But are these things good? Do they do you any good—do they benefit you? Surely, thinks Plato, you are here like a craftsperson with tools and material—they do not do you any good until you put them to *use*, that is, *do* something with them. Moreover, you have to do the *right* thing with them, put them to use which is expert and intelligent, or they will not benefit you—indeed may do you harm. Someone who wins the lottery, for example, may well not be made any happier by just having the money. Unless she puts it to intelligent use, the money may do nothing for her, or even ruin her life. Happiness cannot just be the stuff you have; you have to put it to good use, deal with it in the way that a craftsperson deals with her materials, before it will benefit you, and so make your life better.

Hence we find that the virtues, which enable us to deal well with the material advantages of our life, are called (in the *Laws*) "divine goods," in contrast to the "human goods" constituted by those material advantages. Without the divine goods, we will lose the benefit of the human ones. So the value for us of health, wealth, and the like depends on our possession of virtues like courage and justice. And the virtues depend in turn for their value in a human life on the practical reasoning which forms them and guides their

BALTIMORE LOTTERY—DRAWING THE PRIZES.—SEE PRECEDING PAGE.

According to Plato, happiness cannot be simply having things that people think of as good—winnings from the lottery, for example; you must do something—the right thing—with those winnings for you to benefit from them. In this photographic print from an 1853 wood engraving published in the *Illustrated News*, hopeful lottery ticketholders await the results.

application. Hence in the *Euthydemus* the virtues which make something out of the stuff of our lives are identified with wisdom, the practical intelligence which guides virtuous living.

We obviously have a bold thought here, but just how bold? Is Plato saying that things like health and wealth do not just by their presence make my life better, but do make it better if practical wisdom puts them to good use? If so, he thinks that they are good only conditionally—

The value of our material advantages, such as health and wealth, depends on our possession of the divine goods, such as courage and justice. This detail of a 1508 ceiling fresco by Italian master Raphael in the Room of the Segnatura in the Vatican shows an allegory of Justice holding a sword in her right hand and scales in her left.

only in the context of a well-lived life. Or does he think, more austerely, that things like health and wealth are not good at all, and that it is only the intelligent use I make of health, wealth, and other goods of fortune that makes my life better, while their presence does not?

Plato seems not to have thought through the difference between these positions, since we find language supporting both. Later ethical theories distinguished them, and the second, more austere position, that of the Stoics, was generally thought to have won in claiming Plato as its ancestor. One reason for this is that the more austere view implies that being virtuous is in itself sufficient for a happy life, and this is a position that finds support elsewhere in Plato.

The position that being virtuous itself is sufficient for a happy life is supported by more than one of Plato's works and was espoused by the later philosophical school Stoicism, whose founder, Zeno of Citium (ca. 335–ca. 263 BCE), is pictured here in a bust cast at the Pushkin museum from an original in Naples.

What Matters

In *Apology* (Socrates' defense speech), *Crito*, and *Gorgias* we find explicit statements of a very uncompromising kind. Socrates claims that all that is relevant to the issue of whether someone is happy or not is whether they are virtuous. If we know that a course of action is wrong, then we should not do it, and no amount of anything we could gain or lose by doing the action makes any impact on this point. Even if your life is at risk, you should not try to save it by compromising your values.

• • • • •

UNCOMPROMISING VIRTUE

In the *Crito* (48c–d) Socrates, waiting for execution, examines why he should or should not try to escape from prison.

SOCRATES: We should now examine this—whether it is just for me to try to escape [from prison], or not. If it turns out to be just, let us try, and if not, let's drop it. But these considerations you mention, about spending money, and reputation, and bringing up my children, I suspect, Crito, that these are in truth considerations that appeal to . . . most people. But for us, since the argument demands it, there is nothing else to examine except what we just said, namely, whether we shall be acting justly [if we arrange my escape] or whether we shall in truth be acting unjustly if we do all this. And if this will clearly be an unjust action for us to do, then there is no need at all for us to take into account whether I will have to die if I stay and do nothing, or have to suffer anything else whatever rather than do wrong.

• • • • •

Why is Socrates so sure that the claims of virtue cannot be compromised—cannot indeed be weighed up against considerations like those of money, security, and so on? We have seen that virtue is not just one good thing for me to have, something that might be measured against other good things, such as wealth or security. Rather, virtue is a "divine" good—it is either the only unconditional good, or the only thing which is good at all. And it holds this position because

According to Socrates, all that is relevant to the issue of whether someone is happy is whether he or she is virtuous. This detail of a medieval tapestry is from the book *Zahm und wild, Basler und Straßburger Bildteppiche des 15. Jahrhunderts* (Tame and wild, Basel and Strasbourg tapestries of the fifteenth century); it depicts a virtuous woman using her expertise not only for her own good but for that of others: in taming the mythological figure of the woodwose (wild man) she protects herself from his advances, helps the woodwose himself (by civilizing him, not a controversial goal at the time), and saves other women from being accosted by him.

it is virtue which enables us to put other conventionally good things to good use—hence, it is what makes the difference between having things like health and wealth benefit us or do us no good, or even ruin our lives. Hence virtue is often thought of as a kind of skill or expertise—a kind of practical knowledge which is applied in making materials into a unified and finished product.

The idea here is a powerful one. By the time I start thinking about how to live my life well, I already, as we say, have a life—I have a set of commitments and relationships, such as my family and my job, and a set of goals, my ambitions and dreams. I also, typically, want to be a good person, to be courageous rather than cowardly, fair rather than unjust, and the like. Plato tells us, uncompromisingly, that virtue has a special role, and a special kind of value. To be virtuous is not just to have some goods like wealth, health, and so on, and also virtue. Rather, virtue is the *controlling* and *defining* element in your life; everything else is just materials for it to work on, and it produces a result which is either a well-organized whole or, if it fails, a mess. If we look at things this way, we can appreciate why Plato sees the role of virtue as so crucial in a life. He does not, however, articulate the kind of precise theory that later philosophers did produce as a result of thinking about, and refining, this idea of virtue as the controlling element in a life.

Becoming Like God

This may already strike modern readers as a demanding view. Most of us probably have more sympathy with Aristotle's commonsensical position, which allows that virtue is important as the basic organizing factor in your life, but insists that conventional goods like health and wealth are also good and make your life better if you have them (and, if you lose them, disrupt your life sufficiently that you are no longer happy).

Plato's is without doubt a very demanding position, and was recognized as such in the ancient world (as already indicated, it was generally identified with the austere Stoic position). If he is right, my life should be lived very differently from the way I now live it; instead of pursuing goals like wealth or power I should do all I can to have my life organized and controlled by virtue—and for most people this will make a tremendous difference.

Sometimes, however, we find Plato putting forward the idea that it is not enough to transform your life by getting virtue to direct your priorities. Rather, you should recognize that all our everyday concerns and worries are really petty and unimportant. You should try to take the perspective from which the things that people get worked up about are seen as merely trivial. Virtue requires, in other words, *detachment* from everyday concerns, and hence from the mixture of good and bad that is inevitable in ordinary life. For in life as it is, there is no such thing as really being virtuous, being *perfect*—"that is why we should try to flee as fast as we can from the world here to the world there. This flight is coming to be like god as far as is possible, and this coming to be like god is coming to be just and pious, with understanding" (*Theaetetus* 176a–b.)

The idea of becoming like god would strike Plato's audience as shocking. Gods are a different kind of being from humans, just as the other animals are. Traditionally, for a human to seek to become a god was a transgression (one that the traditional gods were quick to punish). What Plato has in mind is naturally not this, but a philosophically refined view of what god is. God is purely good, wholly without evil (unlike the traditional Greek gods), and to become like god is to aspire to get as near to perfection as a human can.

The ideal of virtue as becoming like god runs against the main current of ancient ethical thought, which takes virtue to be an ideal fulfillment of human nature and its potential, not an attempt to transcend it and to become another kind of being altogether in a quest for perfection that can be attained only in a withdrawal from everyday life. Sidelined for many hundreds of years, the otherworldly ideal had a new lease on life in late antiquity, in the Neoplatonist interpretations of Plato and the impact these had on the intellectual development of Christianity.

Educating Good People

Attracted as he at times is to this idea, however, Plato for the most part thinks of virtue as a *practical* kind of knowledge, exercised in and on the agent's life. Moreover, as we have seen, he thinks that becoming virtuous is crucial for someone hoping to achieve what everyone hopes to achieve, namely, happiness. How, though, is a person to become virtuous? Aristotle, Plato's pupil, later thinks that we start by taking as role models the virtuous people in our community, and proceed to emulate and to criticize the content of their deliberations. If we develop well, we achieve virtue that is richer, more reflective and unified than what we start with; but we will not go far wrong in beginning from our community's standards. Plato wholly disagrees; some of his most vivid passages present the person who aspires to virtue as being quite at odds with their community, finding little sympathy or support for their own ideas. The more talented and sensitive a person is, he suggests in one passage, the more they will be molded by the various kinds of pressure that society brings to bear.

The performance of dramas and epic poetry, such as works by the Greek poet Homer, were to ancient Athenian society what films, television, and books are to us today. Plato took such influential media seriously, refusing to regard them as harmless. This mural painting by a Roman master from the first century BCE depicts a scene from one of Homer's two major works, the *Odyssey*.

Plato recognizes that these pressures are not all of an overtly moral or political kind. What we call a society's culture affects people in lots of ways. In particular, Plato is the first to emphasize the importance of what we call the arts in forming the values of the members of a society. The role played in our society by films, television, and books was played in Plato's Athens by the performance of dramas in the theater, by festivals, and by the learning and performance of various kinds of poetry—epic (notably Homer's *Iliad* and *Odyssey*) and lyric. Plato takes these very seriously, refusing to regard them as mere harmless entertainment.

In the improved city of Plato's *Laws*, in which Plato insists on a complete reform of his society's culture, there is none of the drama that made up such a large part of Greek popular culture (what we now call "Greek tragedy"). Melpomene, the Greek muse of tragedy, is shown holding a tragic mask in this statue from the second century CE.

In two of his longest works, the *Republic* and the *Laws*, the latter a work in which he sketches a legal code for a new city, Plato insists on radical reform of his community's culture, in the interests of the moral growth of its members. The content of traditional culture, notably poetry, is to be thoroughly reformed, and purged of passages which encourage selfish and uncooperative behavior. And Plato is suspicious of the very idea of dramatic representation. He thinks, as have puritans in a number of traditions, that acting parts makes the actor's own self weak and pliable. Moreover, he distrusts the effect of drama on the audience; it encourages them to feel serious emotions lightly, weakening their control over their own emotions. In the improved city of the *Laws* there is none of the drama which made up so large a part of Greek popular culture (and which has come down to us as "Greek tragedy"). Plato is unrepentant about the impoverishment of people's creative and imaginative side; for him what matters is moral development, and the energies on which the arts elsewhere draw are in Plato's ideal community strictly focused on that.

· · · · ·

THE LEVELING EFFECT OF POPULAR OPINION

Plato's distrust of the effects of popular culture in stifling individual thought comes out vividly in this passage from the *Republic* (492a–c).

SOCRATES: The nature of the person who loves wisdom, as we laid it down, will necessarily arrive as it grows at every virtue, if, that is, it gets appropriate teaching. But if it is sown, and nurtured as it grows, in one that is inappropriate, then, unless some god happens to rescue it, it must turn out quite the opposite. Or do you too think what most people do, namely that some young people are corrupted by sophists, and that it's some sophists, private people, who do the corrupting to any great extent? Don't you think that it's the very people who say this who are the greatest sophists of all, and who do the most complete educating, producing people to be the way they want them, young and old, men and women?

When? he said.

When many of them are sitting together in an assembly, the law courts, the theater, the camp or some other general meeting of a lot of people; they make a huge uproar as they criticize some things said or done and praise others—excessively in both cases—by yelling and banging, and as well as them, the rocks and the surrounding place echo the uproar of praise and blame and return it doubled. When things are like this, what heart will a young man have, as the saying goes? What kind of individual education of his will hold out and not be swept away by criticism and praise of this sort, being carried off by the flood wherever it goes, so that he agrees with them about fine and base things, practices what they do, and becomes just like them?

· · · · ·

The Individual and the State

So far I have talked of community rather than state, but for Plato there is no sharp boundary between the cultural and the political. His ideas on how states should be organized reject the idea that politics provides a framework within which individuals can develop as they see best in pursuing their own goals. Indeed, Plato's political ideals are throughout driven by the thought that it is competitive individualism which is the main political problem. People want to "drag" things into their own houses and enjoy whatever they achieve privately, instead of wanting to cooperate in the production of shared goods, which all can enjoy publicly. In an avowedly fantastic sketch of an "ideal state" in the *Republic*, and in a more detailed account in the *Laws* of how a new Greek city could be organized on idealized lines, Plato reforms both political and educational institutions to produce a person whose self-conception will be primarily that of a citizen, someone whose life goals are shared with those of his fellow citizens—and her fellow citizens, for even in the *Laws* Plato thinks that women should think of themselves as citizens, sharing in public space rather than trapped in individual domestic drudgery. In the *Republic* fantasy these ideas go to the lengths of abolishing the nuclear family altogether; in the *Laws* Plato moves rather to strengthening it as a basis for educating a communally minded citizenry.

In Plato's *Republic*, the philosopher bans the nuclear family, but in *Laws*, he strengthens it as a basis for educating a communally minded citizenry. This Greek family scene on a funerary stele is from the third century BCE.

What does Plato think is the justification for such radical ideas, which would alter institutions relentlessly in the interests of producing more socially minded people? This is, he thinks, the only rational way of organizing society so as to function as a whole rather than consisting in a bunch of conflicting individuals. These ideas are always presented as an expert's solution, and constantly compared with the authoritative pronouncements of the expert navigator or doctor. In contrast, democracy, the accepted position in Plato's Athens, is presented as a chaotic scramble of competing voices, each shouting for a selfish individual claim with no expert grasp of the needs of the whole.

· · · · ·

DEMOCRACY AND BUREAUCRACY

Plato sees democracy as imposing stifling bureaucracy on gifted individuals. Here (*Statesman* 298c–299b) he satirically describes what navigation and medicine would be like if run by Athenian democracy. He later admits that democratic control is useful as a safeguard against abuse of power in our actual world.

VISITOR FROM ELEA: So suppose we were to make it our policy . . . no longer to allow [either navigation or medicine] to have full control over anyone, slave or free, but to call ourselves together as an assembly. . . . We permit both laymen and other craftsmen to contribute their opinion about sailing and diseases, as to how we should use drugs and the doctor's instruments on the sick, and even as to ships themselves . . . and when this is written on notice boards and stone blocks . . . this is how for all future time ships are to be sailed and the sick taken care of.

In Plato's *Statesman,* he gives voice to his belief that democracy stifles gifted individuals with bureaucracy. Pictured here is a fragment of a *kleroterion,* an instrument of Athenian democracy by which public offices and juries were filled. In jury selection, for example, citizens' *pinakia* (tokens) were inserted into predetermined slots in the *kleroterion,* and a group of white and black balls was dropped through a tube mounted on the side of the device. A crank device ejected one ball at a time, and its color determined, row by row, who would be chosen for jury duty that day.

YOUNG SOCRATES: What you've described is very peculiar.

VISITOR FROM ELEA: And we'd also set up yearly officials from the people . . . selected by lottery; and these on taking office should fulfill it by steering the ships and curing the sick according to the written rules.

YOUNG SOCRATES: This is even harder to accept.

These *pinakia*, or tokens, housed at the Ancient Agora Museum in Athens, were inserted by citizens into predetermined slots in the *kleroterion*, part of the democratic jury-selection process of ancient Athens.

VISITOR FROM ELEA: Consider also what follows after this. When each official's year ends, courts will have to be set up . . . and ex-officials have to be tried and investigated. Anyone who wants to can accuse one of not steering the ships that year according to the written rules . . . and the same goes for those curing the sick. The court has to assess how those condemned should be punished or pay restitution.

YOUNG SOCRATES: Well, anyone willing voluntarily to hold office in these conditions would fully deserve any punishment and restitution!

• • • • •

As Plato sees it, democracy is a menace because it rejects the idea that society should be directed by expertise, and thus blocks changes that would encourage people to think less individualistically. It drags gifted people down to the lowest level of shared understanding. On the other hand, in the world as it is, the bureaucracy and splitting up of power that democracy encourages do prevent abuse of power by uncontrolled, misguided individuals who merely think that they are experts. In the *Republic* fantasy, absolute power is given to perfect people. But in other works where Plato is thinking more about actual conditions the expert ruler remains an ideal, but democracy is accepted, unenthusiastically, as the best working option. In the *Laws* the institutions of Athenian democracy are taken over as a basis

The Pnyx (ruins shown here in a recent photograph) was the seat of democracy in ancient Athens. It was the site of the ecclesia, the popular assembly, where Athenian citizens who had the right to vote (Athenian-born men over the age of eighteen) met periodically to conduct public business.

to be modified in a community-minded direction; no other kind of institution is envisaged as a place to start. For Plato, democracy is the worst form of government except for all the others. Only in an ideal world could we do better, and live not merely alongside one another but together, with shared lives and ideals. Plato is, as we have seen, utterly uncompromising about the individual's commitment to virtue, whatever the state of the actual world. But he also thinks, more or less hopefully, that the actual world could be improved in the interests of virtue.

SIX

My Soul and Myself

•

Problems About the Soul

In Greek thought, the soul (*psyche*) is what causes living things (*empsucha*) to be alive. This leaves a large range of questions about the soul open. Our bodies are animated; is what animates them itself some kind of physical body, or is it something of an entirely different kind? If the latter, how is its nature to be understood? Is the soul indissolubly united to the body it animates, so that at death it perishes when the body ceases to be animated—or could it carry on in some other form? Am I the animated body, or am I really to be identified with the soul

One of the questions posed in Greek thought is whether the soul is indissolubly united to the body, so that when the body dies the soul dies with it. This painting by Dutch artist Hieronymus Bosch (ca. 1450–1516), which appeared in *The Smithsonian Institution: An Establishment for the Increase and Diffusion of Knowledge Among Men*, by Walter Karp, shows a miser on his deathbed between an angel and Death, who entreat the miser for his soul.

Plato was a model of dualism when it came to thought about the body and the soul; he believed they were two completely separate entities. This late-nineteenth-century lithograph, *Dr. Alford's Biblical Chart of Man*, contains an "explanatory key showing the relation of the soul to the body, the senses to the attributes, mortality to immortality."

rather than with the animated body? If so, is there some sense in which *I* could survive death, the cessation of the body's animation?

By Plato's time there had been a variety of answers to these questions, and his works appear at first to offer a spread of answers themselves, not always consistently. On two points he always appears firm. He always takes as a starting point the thought that the soul is a different kind of thing from the body. Indeed, he is often regarded as a paradigm of dualism, the position that soul and body (in modern versions mind and body) are radically different kinds of entity. Further, Plato never doubts that when I ask what I, myself, really am, the answer will be that I am my soul, rather than my animated body. Hence Socrates, on his deathbed, jokingly reminds his friends that they will not be burying *him*, only his body.

· · · · ·

SOCRATES ON HIS DEATHBED

In the *Phaedo* (115c–116a) Socrates prepares to drink the hemlock:

"How shall we bury you?" asked Crito.

"However you like," Socrates said, "—if you catch me and I don't get away from you." He laughed quietly and said, looking at us, "See, I can't convince Crito that what *I* am is Socrates here, the person talking to you now and drawing up the arguments. He thinks that I am what he will shortly see as a corpse, and asks how he shall bury me. I seem to have wasted my words on him, though consoling both you and myself, in the argument I have long been making, that when I drink the poison I shall no longer remain here with you, but will go away to some kind of happiness of the blessed. . . . You must cheer up, and say that you are burying my body, and bury it however you like and in what you think is the most customary way."

$$\bullet \bullet \bullet \bullet \bullet$$

But Plato appears to offer different and sometimes conflicting answers to further questions about the soul. Sometimes he insists that the soul is a simple nature, while in other passages we find that it is divided, indeed has parts which are metaphorically represented as individual humans and animals. Sometimes what is essential to the soul appears to be its power of thinking and reasoning; sometimes it is the power of self-motion. And, while Plato in general defends the idea that the soul is immortal, so that its relation to the body is merely temporary, we find conflicting suggestions about the nature of this relation. Sometimes the soul appears as the body's ruler and director; sometimes as its unhappily trapped prisoner.

There is no one consistent account, however general, uniting everything that Plato says about the soul. Some scholars have pointed to this as evidence for development in Plato's thought, but it is difficult to find a single line of development here. It is more natural to find in Plato several lines of inquiry which have common themes but do not always turn out to lead in the same direction.

Simple or Complex?

One of the most famous passages in Plato is his division of the soul into three "parts" or aspects in the *Republic*. As an animated body, I function as a unity, but I contain distinct sources of motivation, something which becomes apparent when they conflict. Plato imagines a thirsty person who desires to drink but refrains, because drinking would be bad for him. (The reason is not specified; there are many ways in which it might be bad for him.) This is not simply the kind of conflict that arises from wanting to do two things in time adequate for only one of them. Rather, the conflict here is between two different *kinds* of motivation; desire just goes for what I want *now*, without regard for what will happen later, whereas the motivation to refrain comes from a realization of what is good for me over time. This is *reason*, which enables me to grasp and understand the idea of my life as a whole, and which motivates me to pursue this, notably by opposing desires whose gratification would interfere with it.

Reason is not just an intellectual faculty that can work out what is best for you overall, as a person with a continuing life, a past and a future. It also motivates you without the help of desire. Desire moves you to get its object *here and now*; reason is what gets you to resist this gratification when it is not in your best interests overall.

The contrast between short-term desires and long-term reasoned motivation is clear enough, but Plato does not find it adequate as an explanation of all of our behavior. There is also *thumos*, which is variously translated as "spirit," "the passionate part," and the like. It is distinguished from reason by the fact that it can be inarticulate, as in children and animals, and it can also come into conflict with desires. Plato has picked on the interesting point that we can sometimes overrule particular desires without having an articulate rationale for so doing. Sometimes we are motivated by a sense of self which is unified and responsive to ideals and aspirations that conflict with particular desires, without being able to reason out the basis for this. (Soldiers responding to their country's need form one of Plato's examples.)

This is the part of the soul where we find emotions, more complex and cognitively responsive than desires but falling short of the reflective abilities of reason.

In the *Republic* the main function of the theory of the soul's parts is to show that the good life is one in which reason rules the whole soul, allowing each part to flourish as it should. Reason's rule is justified by its grasp of the good of the whole person, while the other parts grasp only their own good, and therefore lead to dysfunction if they are in charge of the whole.

We find the same model in the *Phaedrus*, where the person is depicted as a two-horse chariot whose driver, reason, tries to control the force of two horses, one (spirit) cooperative and one (desire) which tries to rebel and drag the whole chariot in the wrong direction.

Although spirit and desire are here battling animal forces, we also find that they communicate in language. Plato represents them as talking horses (one of which is deaf!). He is thinking of the soul's parts both as conflicting forces with varying strengths, and also as aspects of a person which are all responsive to reason in varying degrees. Spirit and desire are rational enough to communicate, but not rational enough to be depicted in human form. In the *Timaeus* the soul's parts are located in different parts of the body, in ways which encourage reason (in the head) to dominate spirit (in the upper body) and desire (in the lower body).

In the *Republic*, Plato divides the soul into three parts, or aspects. The first is desire, *epithumia*, the pursuit of what the individual wants now. This is sometimes represented by the ancient Greeks as Pothos, god of longing, yearning, and desire. It is countered by reason, represented by the ancient Greeks as Athena, goddess of wisdom and reason, which understands the long-term ramifications of our choices and persuades us to resist immediate gratification. This marble statue of Pothos is a Roman copy after a Greek original from around 300 BCE; Athena is shown in a marble statue, a Roman copy after a Greek original of the late fifth century BCE.

The description in the *Phaedrus* of the soul as a winged two-horse chariot, strange as it is, has proved attractive to artists throughout the centuries. Here we find it on a medallion worn by the subject of a portrait bust by Donatello (1386–1466). It identifies the subject as interested in the revived Platonism (greatly influenced by the later ancient school of Neoplatonism) which was influential in Renaissance Italy.

We also, however, find in the *Phaedo* (78b–84b) and toward the end of the *Republic* arguments which actually depend on the position that the soul is a *simple* unity. Both arguments claim that the soul is immortal, and that this would be impossible if its true nature were composite. The underlying thought is that anything composed of distinguishable parts is liable to dissolution into those parts; and if what is so liable will be dissolved at some point it cannot be immortal. (This thought can of course be challenged.) How does this idea relate to the soul's division into "parts"? Since both occur in one dialogue, the

In Plato's *Timaeus*, the soul's three parts are located in different parts of the body: the reason in the head, the spirit in the upper body, and desire in the lower body. Shown here is a page from the *Timaeus* from the 1578 Stephanus edition of Plato's works.

If the soul's true nature is to be unaffected by the body, then what animated Socrates' living body will not survive Socrates' death; only the aspects that are unaffected by the body will survive. This depiction of the dead Socrates is by nineteenth-century Russian sculptor Mark Antokolski.

Republic, it is to be hoped that they can be reconciled, and this seems to be the purpose of the phrase "its true nature." What makes the soul even apparently divided is its association with the body. It is the soul's embodiment (a problematic relation, we shall find) which explains how our motivations can be conflicted; the soul itself is not affected by divisions which arise from the nature of our existence as animated bodies.

If the soul's true nature is to be unaffected by the body, however, then what is it that survives Socrates' death? It will not be what animated Socrates' living body, but only the aspects of that which are unaffected by the body. Should Socrates be so sure that this will be *his* survival?

Mind or Mover?

Plato tends to contrast the soul with the body; in describing our psychological life and quest for knowledge he often sees these as competing forces, always to the disadvantage of the body. This is one reason why his ideas appealed to the ascetic church fathers, who interpreted the scriptural contrast of spirit and flesh as the Platonic contrast of sharply opposed soul and body, thus having a drastic effect on Western Christianity's attitude to the body.

We have seen, though, that the soul is not simply opposed to the body; when it animates the body, parts of it are in some way affected by and involved with the body. So, while sometimes Plato refers simply to the ordinary contrast between the body and what animates it, in other passages what he has in mind is the contrast between the *animated*, ensouled body and the aspect of the soul which is unaffected by the body. In some passages about knowledge this contrast is developed as a contrast between the senses and the soul; the senses give us information, but the soul is stimulated not just to receive and process this information but to reflect on it and go beyond it. In the *Republic* (523a–525b) the soul finds that the senses give mutually conflicting reports and is stimulated to reflect on what an adequate grasp of the world would require. In the *Theaetetus* (184c–186e) Socrates gets young Theaetetus to discover for himself that the senses on their own cannot account for the way that we not only take in sensory information but interpret it and go beyond it.

· · · · ·

PERCEPTION, BODY, AND MIND

SOCRATES: Take hot, hard, light and sweet—do you think that each of the things by which you perceive these belongs to the body? . . . And are you also ready to agree that when you perceive something through one power, it's impossible to perceive it through another? For example, you can't perceive by sight what you perceive through hearing, and vice versa?

THEAETETUS: How could I not be ready to agree to that?

SOCRATES: So, if you think something about both of them, you wouldn't be having a perception about both of them through either one of these instruments?

THEAETETUS: No.

SOCRATES: Take a sound and a color. First, don't you think *this* about them, that both of them *are*?

THEAETETUS: Yes.

SOCRATES: And that each of them is different from the other one, and the same as itself?

THEAETETUS: Of course.

SOCRATES: And that both together are two, and each is one?

THEAETETUS: That too.

SOCRATES: And you are capable of investigating whether they are unlike each other, or like each other?

THEAETETUS: I suppose so.

SOCRATES: Well, through what is it that you think all these things about them? It isn't through hearing or through sight either that you can grasp what's common to them. . . . Through what does the power work which makes clear to you what is common to everything, including these things, to which we apply the words "is" and "is not" and the others we just used in the questions? What instruments are you going to assign to all these through which the perceiving aspect of us perceives all of them?

THEAETETUS: You mean being and not being, and likeness and unlikeness, and same and different, and one and any other number they have. And clearly you're also asking about odd and even and everything that

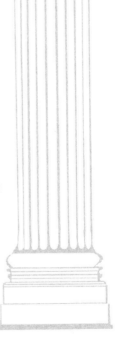

follows them, and asking through what bodily instrument we perceive these with the soul. . . . Well, really, Socrates, I couldn't say, except that it seems to me that they just don't have their own instrument the way the others do; the soul seems to me to consider the things that are common to everything itself, through itself.

SOCRATES: Theaetetus . . . you've saved me a lengthy argument, since it seems to you that the soul considers some things itself, through itself, and others through the body's powers. That was what I thought myself, but I wanted you to believe it too.

(Theaetetus 184e–185e)

· · · · ·

There is difficulty in sorting out a consistent overall account of just what in our sensory judgments Plato ascribes to the body and what to the soul working through the body, but one thing is quite clear from such passages: the soul here is what we would now call the mind or understanding. Our psychological resources include not just the ability to take in sensory information about the world, but the distinct cognitive ability to unify and make sense of it. Moreover, the understanding is not limited to interpreting the senses; its reflections lead it to go beyond what the senses provide and to discover objects that it can grasp without the senses. Such independent working of the mind is often opposed in the sharpest terms to our sensory experience. They are seen as competing for psychological

It is not always clear which of our sensory experiences Plato attributes to the body and which to the soul working through the body. This depiction of the sense of taste is one of a five-part series of engravings by Dutch engraver Jan Saenredam (1565–1607).

space and energy, and reliance on the senses is disparaged as passive dozing along, while for the person to wake up is for her to start using her mind independently of what sense experience provides. Some of Plato's most vivid passages disparage the body and reliance on it for knowledge: this is called dreaming, as opposed to waking up.

One important point frequently stressed about the objects of this kind of pure thinking is that they are stable and unchanging. They are the objects of mathematics and what Plato calls Forms, to which we shall return in the next chapter. In the *Phaedo* there is even a passage (78b–84b) in which we find Socrates emphasizing that the soul is akin to the unchanging Forms, the objects of pure thought which are unaffected by any of the sources of change in the world of our sensory experience. The soul's immortality is inferred from its likeness to its unchanging, stable, and simple objects—objects of pure thought and understanding.

However, in the *Phaedrus* (245c–246a) we find that the soul is said to be immortal because it is always in motion (or change), and that its motion never fails because it moves itself, while everything else is moved by it. The argument is about "all soul," and this introduces a difficulty: it is not clear whether this means every individual soul, or soul as a kind of stuff—"soul" being used as a mass term like "snow" or "gold" which picks out not individuals but quantities or amounts of something. Certainly when we find related ideas in the *Timaeus* and *Laws* (893b–899d) we also find that the world as a whole has a soul, of which our souls are individual portions; so Plato has at least moved his main focus away from the individual ensouled person.

The idea that what defines the soul is self-motion is a deep and interesting one, which Aristotle was to develop further. It is, after

Plato's idea that what defines the soul is self-motion was picked up and developed further by his student Aristotle, leading him eventually to his idea of the unmoved mover. This image of Aristotle is from the *Nuremberg Chronicle*.

all, an obvious fact about living, as opposed to nonliving, things that their sources of motion and change are internal to them. Further, with the thought that all other kinds of motion require a self-mover to account for them, Plato makes the first start in an argument which leads eventually to Aristotle's idea of an *unmoved* mover. It is clear, however, that in arguing to the soul's immortality from its self-motion Plato is thinking of a different aspect of the soul from that where he argued to its immortality from its likeness to unchanging objects. Clearly it is our intellect which Plato is taking to be akin to its unmoving objects, and this is not the soul which is always in motion. Further, these are not just different aspects of my individual embodied soul. Rather, Plato develops two very different ideas of what characterizes the soul as opposed to the body. It is my soul which enables me to aspire to knowledge that is beyond what sensory experience can provide. But my soul is also a portion of a cosmic force which is itself actively in motion. Later Platonists found more or less academic ways of reconciling these strands of thought; Plato never does this in the dialogues.

Ruler or Prisoner?

The soul, we often find, stands to the body as ruler to ruled; it is the body's superior and its organizing principle. Rulers need subjects and (Plato thinks) vice versa; this looks like a stable, if unequal, relationship. Yet we also find, notably in the *Phaedo*, that we should try to "purify" ourselves from the body, and that philosophy is to be properly understood as practice for dying, the soul's final escape from the prison of the body. The body is an evil which drags the soul down, pestering it with its needs; death is a welcome release for the soul from its infection by the body.

The conflicts we find here come from emphasis and rhetoric rather than substance. Plato always thinks that soul and body are fundamentally unlike entities, and he has different, vivid ways of bringing this out. One is to represent the body as a hindrance to the soul; another is to emphasize the soul's activities as guiding the body. These are different ways of laying stress on what has for good reason

Plato follows two lines of thought in his discussion of the relationship between the body and the soul, one assigning the soul the role of ruler over the body, the other representing the body as a hindrance to the soul. This romantic lithograph published by Currier & Ives in 1876 espouses the second line of thought. The verse below the image reads, "I will sing you a song of that beautiful land. / The far away home of the soul. / Where no storms ever beat on the glittering strand. / While the years of eternity roll. / Oh, that home of the soul in my visions and dreams. / Its bright jasper walls I can see; Till I fancy but thinly the veil intervenes / Between this fair city and me."

come to be called "Platonic dualism": the idea that soul and body are such different kinds of entity that their relation is problematic and difficult to understand. But Plato makes things harder for us, and for himself, than he needs, by failing to focus on just where the line distinguishing soul from body should be drawn. As we have seen, sometimes the contrast is between the body to be animated and what animates it, sometimes between the animated body and either intellectual functions or a power of self-motion, belonging to the soul over and above its embodiment. It is because this line shifts, as well as because his conception of the soul's nature is not always constant, that we find such diverging pictures of the soul-body relation.

Reincarnation, Myth, and Argument

One of the most strongly marked themes in the dialogues is that the soul survives the person's death; but we have seen that it is not clear what this soul is. Especially where the emphasis is on leaving the body behind, it is hard to see how what survives could be the individual soul—Socrates' soul, say—for everything pertaining to the history of Socrates as an embodied individual will have been shed. How can Socrates' soul retain its individuality while retaining none of this history?

Plato struggles with this issue rather than resolving it. In some dialogues we find stories of postmortem judgment, with rewards for virtuous lives and punishments for the wicked. These rewards and punishments, moreover, are often said to have an effect on the soul with respect to further lives it will live in an embodied state. Sometimes we get a full-blown story of reincarnation, present lives being the fruit of past lives and having within themselves consequences for future lives. All this presupposes that

In his dialogues, Plato makes clear that an individual's soul survives his or her death. What is not clear is what the soul in fact is. Plato struggles with rather than resolves this issue, bringing the ideas of both reincarnation and judgment into his work. Plato, of course, was not the only philosopher to develop a line of thinking on reincarnation. This Buddhist reincarnation wheel, which outlines the cycle of reincarnation, and is held in the clutches of Mara, Lord of Death and Desire, was built sometime between 1177 and 1249.

an individual soul can remain one and the same soul through many lives, capable of improvement or degeneration as a result of them (though not, of course, conscious of them when in the embodied state).

The status of these judgment and reincarnation stories in Plato is very disputed. Some have hailed these narrative "myths" as poetic invocations of insights that go beyond argument; others have seen them as ways of introducing ideas which evade argument. It is likely that they do not all have the same tone, or function. Some seem ironic (particularly when describing humans as reincarnated as animals), others quite serious.

We should remember that Plato avoids presenting his ideas as dogma, in treatises; he employs various strategies of indirectness. Clearly the idea of a judgment after death on the way a life has been lived was important to him, as was the idea of one life as a fitting outcome of the way another life has been lived. The stories illustrating these ideas can be interpreted as vivid ways of stressing the ethical importance of the way we live now, or as indicating, though not arguing for, a particular metaphysical view of the soul and the self.

Or, of course, as both. Plato's way of writing leaves us to extract ideas from different dialogues, put them together, and work out his position on a given issue. This can leave us frustrated, nowhere more so than with his views on the soul. We will be less frustrated if we think of him as coming up with different kinds of answers as he keeps returning to the nature of the soul. He never doubts that the soul is so different a kind of thing from the body that their relationship is problematic. Nor does he doubt that the soul is immortal—that in some way what I really am is not given by the boundaries of my embodied human life. His explorations of the soul's nature do not all go in the same direction because Plato, while sticking firmly to some points, follows more than one argument about the soul where it leads, and seeks truth about difficult issues rather than attempting to arrive at a tidy finished position.

SEVEN

The Nature of Things

•

Chaos and Order

The natural world, despite disruptions, displays a striking degree of order and regularity. For Plato the best model for understanding it is to think of it as a product made by a craftsman, who does the best job he can in imposing order on otherwise unruly materials.

In the *Timaeus* Plato describes the creation of the world as work done by a divine Craftsman, who does the job by reference to a model—a system of rational principles which are to be embodied in materials to produce a unified result. To the extent that the world can be seen to display rational structure, we can understand it as being the work of Reason; to the extent that it is embodied in materials

For Plato, the best way to understand the natural world is as a product made by a craftsman. This illustration from William Blake's *Europe: A Prophecy* (1794) depicts God as an architect creating the world.

According to Plato, God not only created order from chaos—as depicted in this 1731 illustration by engraver Bernard Picart, showing the heavens in chaos at the origin of the world, with constellations (including the twelve signs of the zodiac), fire, clouds, and wind—but created only *good* from that chaos.

which constrain reason and make failures possible, we have to take into account the effects of what Plato calls Necessity, the way things just have to be, whether there is a good reason for it or not.

Plato's account, fanciful in detail and often obscure, raises a number of issues about what we would call his metaphysics. The divine Craftsman creates a *good* world; why? Mathematics plays an important role in the *Timaeus*'s account of the world's structure—what role does this play in Plato's view both of the world and of the kind of knowledge that we might achieve of it? And finally, the *Timaeus* makes prominent one of Plato's most famous ideas, that the real world is not, as we uncritically take it to be, the world around us that our senses report to us; the real world is rather what we grasp in thought when exercising our minds in abstract philosophical argument, in particular arguments which lead to what Plato calls Forms.

The *Timaeus* was seen as central to Plato's metaphysical thinking until the nineteenth century, when obsession with Plato's political thinking replaced it by the *Republic*, still Plato's most frequently read work. As often with Plato, both works are important, and point up different aspects of his thinking in ways that encourage both unification and contrast.

God and Goodness

The Craftsman God made the best world possible because he is good (*Timaeus* 29d–30c) and so wanted what he made to be as good as it could be. And, being free of jealousy because he is good, he wanted the world, in being as good as it could be, to be as much like him as it could be.

Coming to this idea under the influence of two thousand years of

In a dramatic departure from the beliefs of his own culture, Plato tells us in *Timaeus* that because God is free of jealousy, he made the world as good as it could be. German painter Albrecht Dürer's oil on wood, created around 1504, shows Christ blessing the world.

monotheism (Judaism, Christianity, Islam), we may be unsurprised by the idea that God is good and that his creation is good because he is. Here we should remember two points. One is that Plato is going out on a limb in his own culture. The other is that even so, Plato's position is in an important way still weaker than the monotheistic views we are accustomed to.

Ancient popular religion—various forms of polytheism—did not claim that God, or the gods, were good. This would have seemed naive and unrealistic; the divine, superhuman forces in the world, and in humans, appear to present a mixture of good and bad. The Greek gods of popular religion are capable of petty and destructive behavior. They are, moreover, extremely jealous where humans are concerned.

Plato's idea that God is good, and produces only good, is one that alienates him decisively from popular religion. He never rejects the forms and practices of the religion he knew, but he develops a theology which is radically at odds with most people's understanding of that religion. In the *Republic* he insists that the gods are responsible only for good, and accepts that in a well-organized society this will require a radical censorship of most of the popular stories that people tell about the gods. (As we have seen, Plato does not care about suppressing people's creative and imaginative thinking, in this case about the divine.)

In the *Laws*, he goes further. Although public religion remains that of an ordinary Greek city-state, repressive measures are introduced that have no parallel in the ancient pagan world. Citizens are to have no private shrines or worship of their own; the standard public rites are to be the only ones they take part in. And it matters not just what they do but what they believe; all citizens are to believe that there really are gods, that these gods care for humans, and that they cannot be bribed to overlook wrongdoing. Citizens who deny these beliefs are to be re-educated, or, if unpersuadable, executed. Plato is unique among ancient philosophers in holding it important for everyone to have the right beliefs about God (or the gods) and for

these beliefs prominently to include the belief that God is responsible only for good, not for evil.

No other ancient philosopher rejects popular religion to this extent, and it is no surprise that ancient Christian thinkers found Plato by far the most congenial of the pagan philosophers. His concern with ordinary people's beliefs about God, or the gods, was as important to them as his insistence that God, or the gods, are good, and in no way evil.

The Greek gods of Plato's culture were capable of petty and destructive behavior. In one myth, the mortal hero Actaeon saw Artemis, the goddess of the hunt, at her bath. The goddess was so angry that the mortal had seen her naked that she turned him into a stag, upon which he was killed by his own hounds. This sculpture of Actaeon, half man, half stag, is in the gardens of the magnificent Royal Palace at Caserta in Italy.

Yet there is a barrier separating Plato from later Jews and Christians who took over much of his thought, and in particular spent huge amounts of energy in trying to assimilate the *Timaeus* to the creation story in *Genesis*.

Plato's God is a workman who does the best he can with the materials he has to work with; he creates order from chaos, but he does not create the original materials from nothing. (An already long

In Plato's *Laws*, we learn that the philosopher thinks that citizens should participate only in public rites and have no private shrines of their own, and that they must believe both that there are gods and that the gods care for humans. This view of the temple of Hephaestus and Athena Ergane, dedicated to the patron-god of metalworking and the patron-goddess of pottery and crafts, respectively, and inaugurated in 416–15 BCE, is from an 1851 engraving by Henry Winkles.

tradition in Greek philosophy held that creation from nothing was an incoherent idea.) As a result, Plato does not face the "problem of evil" troubling the Judeo-Christian tradition; if God creates the world from nothing, then why does he create evil as part of it? Plato's God is a creator in the way a craftsman is; he makes the product, which is an excellent one, but he is not responsible for the effects of "Necessity," the unavoidable defects of the materials.

Mathematics and Knowledge

In the *Timaeus* great emphasis is placed on the mathematically calculable nature of the heavenly bodies' motions, even the apparently irregular ones. Plato also sustains the by then familiar view that there are four basic elements, but adds that their mutual transformations are due to the different geometrical figures in their underlying structure. For Plato it is basic to our world's being an ordered one that mathematics is the key to it.

In many dialogues mathematics is an important model for Plato for understanding knowledge. Sometimes, especially in the shorter dialogues where Socrates is depicted examining various types of virtue, the model for having knowledge is that of having a skill or expertise, and what is at issue is *practical* knowledge. Nonetheless, some conditions emerge which for Plato always hold of knowledge (as discussed in Chapter 1). Knowledge can be communicated, and the person with knowledge can "give an account," explain and justify what she knows. And knowledge requires using your mind to think for yourself about things, rather than taking over opinions second-hand without examining them. In contrast, beliefs, even if true, are inferior in at least two ways. They can be produced by "persuasion," techniques for producing conviction which bypass explanation and justification, and result in a person's holding a view without understanding. The person with knowledge, however, understands what he knows and can "give an account" of it. In some works Plato thinks of this giving of an account as being comparable to the articulation an expert could give of her practical expertise.

Mathematics, however, takes hold as a model where Plato puts more stress on two features of knowledge. One is the idea of knowledge as *structured*, not just a mass of information but an organized system of basic truths and others derived from them. To Plato, this ideal of systematization, allowing deployment of what there was to be understood, could be seen in geometry, the best-developed branch of mathematics that he knew. In geometry we can

In the *Timaeus,* Plato trusts in the mathematical calculability of the heavenly bodies. This seventeenth-century engraving depicts Polish astronomer Johannes Hevelius and his assistant using a six-foot sextant to measure the angular distances between stars.

discern the starting points, the derived results, and a transparent account of the way they were derived. This ideal of knowledge appears in the *Meno* and *Phaedo*, but is seen at its most ambitious in the central books of the *Republic*. And in works like the *Timaeus* and *Philebus* we find Plato insisting that it is mathematics which provides us with whatever is organized and reliable in our knowledge.

The second impressive point about mathematics is quite simply its objects. When we learn Pythagoras's theorem, we are grasping something in our thinking, which is not made true (or false) by the particular diagrams we draw to illustrate it; any irregularities in these are irrelevant to the mathematical truth. Although it is not to be encountered in the world of experience, it is certain; having proved it, we know it to be true. It is clear that Plato was deeply impressed by this feature of mathematics: not only can we be certain of the results we prove, we realize that it is only by exercising a certain kind of abstract thinking that we can understand them. We learn that the evidence of our senses may be irrelevant to the results we can prove in thought, which may even conflict with them. For Plato this is the beginning of philosophical wisdom, the right way to think for ourselves about things. Although his views about knowledge vary, and he sometimes thinks that we can know items of experience (compare Chapter 1), Plato is sympathetic to the idea that progress toward knowledge properly begins when we come to think of the world of our experience as irrelevant, and appreciate that it is abstract thinking that produces understanding. Mathematics is a powerful influence on him as an excellent example of this progress.

However, both in its objects and in its way of thinking, mathematics is itself inferior to, and thus merely a good preparation for, the thinking done by the people Plato calls philosophers.

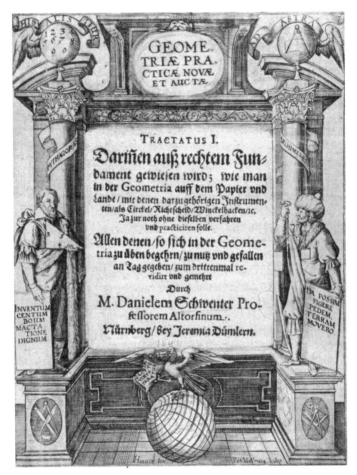

Greek philosopher and mathematician Pythagoras (ca. 580–ca. 500 BCE) is pictured here with Greek mathematician and inventor Archimedes (ca. 287–212 BCE) on the title page of a geometry and surveying manual. Pythagoras holds a right triangle, illustrating his theorem that the square of the length of the hypotenuse of a triangle is equal to the sum of the squares of the other two sides, a piece of knowledge that, once we have possessed it, we know to be true, even though we will not encounter it in the world of experience. *Geometriae practicae novae et auctae* (New and enlarged practical geometry), by mathematician Daniel Schwenter (1585–1636), was published posthumously in 1641.

The Forms

Philosophers, according to Plato, employ a kind of thinking which he calls *dialectic*. His account of what this is differs strikingly in different works, but one aspect remains: it develops in *dialegesthai*, discussion. Philosophy always involves argument and discussion, ideally with others, and requires you to be able to defend your position against the arguments of others. It is not obvious what the best methods are for philosophers to use, and this is where we find the most variation, but again Plato is always sure that philosophical thinking is superior to all other kinds. Even mathematicians do not genuinely understand their own results; it is philosophers who make use of, and examine, others' results to make sense of them and establish the kind of justification they require. This conception of philosophy, which sounds astonishingly arrogant to others, has been one many philosophers aspire to, in spite of periods when philosophy has been bound in advance to answer to the discoveries of science, or theology.

The most famous aspect of Plato's view of philosophy has generally been his claim that philosophical thinking grasps what he calls "Forms" (though he has no technical term, often using a Greek idiom, "the F itself," which conveys little in English). Sometimes his philosophy is presented as though Forms were the high point and centerpiece, which is a tribute to the power of the idea, since Plato, in keeping with the way he writes in the dialogue form, has no sustained presentation of any "theory" of Forms. Forms appear at various points in the dialogues as an idea already familiar to Socrates and others, but there is no positive introduction of this idea, supposed to be so familiar. In the first part of the *Parmenides*, however, six serious objections are brought against Forms, with the conclusion that the idea is a good one but needs further work to be viable.

According to Plato, philosophy always involves argument and discussion and requires you to be able to defend your position against the arguments of others. This image from the fourteenth-century *Liber de herbis* (Book of herbs), by Monfredo de Monte Imperiali, shows an imaginary debate between twelfth-century Spanish-Arab philosopher and physician Averroës and third-century Phoenician Neoplatonic philosopher Porphyry.

The oblique and scanty appearances of Forms have not stopped readers from building a "Theory of Forms" out of these few passages, and from confronting this theory (successfully or not) with Plato's own criticisms. This is probably what Plato wanted us to do, but we should be cautious about making definite or final claims about an idea which is deliberately presented in such an elusive way.

In the *Timaeus* Forms are presented in a very general way, as implied by our recognition of the differences between knowledge and true belief. (Plato, we should notice, does not consider the option that our conception of knowledge might not answer to anything; he assumes that the knowledge we aspire to have is, at least in principle, attainable.) This, however, leaves wide open what kind of thing Forms are, and Plato's treatments are not easy to unify.

In the *Timaeus* itself Forms function as patterns for the Craftsman as he makes our world. Things in our world—species and kinds of thing, and the four primary elements—are embodied in matter and spatially situated (Plato is very obscure on this point, and was criticized for this by Aristotle) and, crucially, they "come to be," whereas Forms

In Plato's *Parmenides*, six serious objections are brought against Forms. The *Parmenides* is a discussion between Socrates and the philosophers Parmenides of Elea, shown here in a ca. fifth-century BCE bust, and Zeno of Elea.

"are, without coming to be." This is the important metaphysical difference between Forms on the one hand and, on the other, the items around us which are said to "participate in" Forms, or to be "likenesses" or "images" of them. This difference is stressed forcibly also in the *Phaedo*, *Republic*, and *Symposium*, in some of Plato's most memorable passages. But we do not always get the same answer to the question of what it is for items in our world to "come to be," and, correspondingly, to the question of what items are "participants" in Forms.

· · · · ·

THE FORMS

TIMAEUS: Now it's with argument that we should make these distinctions and inquire about them. So: is there such a thing as Fire itself by itself, and so on for all the things of which we always say that each is "itself by itself"? Or are the things we see, and whatever we perceive through the body, the only things that have this kind of reality, and is there nothing else at all in any way over and beyond them, so that our claim in each case that there is a thinkable form for each of them is lost labor, nothing after all but words?

The four primary elements, as described by Greek pre-Socratic philosopher Empedocles, are earth, air, fire, and water, as pictured here in a colored woodcut from a 1472 edition of Lucretius's *De rerum natura* (On the nature of things).

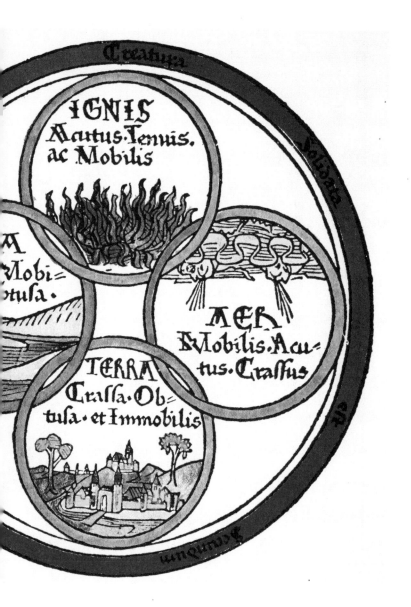

Well, it is not appropriate for us either to dismiss the present question without judgment or verdict, simply insisting that things *are* like this, or to throw into an already long discourse a digression itself lengthy. But if a large distinction drawn briefly could be presented, that would be most suitable of all.

So this is how I myself cast my vote. If understanding and true belief are two different kinds, then absolutely there are these things "by themselves," forms that are not perceivable by us, only thinkable. But if, as some think, true belief is not at all different from understanding, then we have to take everything we perceive through the body as being the most stable items. But we *do* have to say that they are two different things, because they come into being separately, and are unlike each other. We come to have understanding through teaching, while true belief is brought about in us by persuasion. Understanding always involves a true account, while true belief has no account to give. Understanding is not movable by persuasion, while true belief can be changed by it. And we have to say that everybody has a share of true belief, while of understanding only the gods do, and the human race to a small extent.

(Timaeus 51b–e)

· · · · ·

One surprisingly common answer is definitely wrong, namely that there is a Form for every word that we apply to a number of individuals, and so a Form for every general term (making Forms into what were later called universals). This view is based on a mistranslation of a passage in the *Republic* (596a), which actually says that wherever there is a Form there is only one. The principle of a Form for every general term would be completely trivial, and make it baffling why Forms are objects of understanding, items we have to use our minds, with effort, to grasp. Moreover, it runs against Plato's firm view that our use of language embodies convention and prejudice and on its own is no good guide to philosophical truth (*Cratylus*, *Statesman* 262–63).

"Participants" "come to be," while Forms "are." One way in which things come to be is that they change; at one time a thing has one property, and later it comes to have another, and may even come to have a property excluding or opposed to the original one. Certainly it is not hard to find passages where Plato stresses the mutability of the world we experience around us, contrasting this to the changelessness of the Forms. And this connects with understanding; we have a better grasp of what a thing is if we are not forced to characterize it in ways that have to be changed as it changes. (And one feature of mathematics is that its truths do not change over time.) But the mere fact that things around us change is a remarkably weak reason for insisting on their metaphysical inferiority to items that do not change. Fortunately it is not Plato's only reason.

More interesting is the "argument from opposites," which is the most prominent way in which Forms are discussed in the *Phaedo*, *Republic*, and *Hippias Major*. This focuses on the point that, while we can make a true claim that something in the world of our experience is F, for some property F, we can also find some perspective from which we can also claim truly that it is the opposite of F. Sticks which are equal, say, in length are also unequal in, say, width; a

While we can truly claim that something in our world of experience is F, for some property F, we can also find a perspective from which we can truly claim that it is the opposite of F. For example, a girl who is beautiful among other girls is unappealing compared to goddesses. This fragment of a fresco from the Villa Lemmi near Florence, Italy, showing the woman Giovanna degli Albizi with Venus and the Graces, was created between 1486 and 1490.

girl who is beautiful among other girls is unappealing compared to goddesses; an action which is right in being the fulfilling of a promise is also wrong in being irresponsibly dangerous; and so on. Sometimes the perspective from which we find the opposite property to F is far-fetched in the extreme, but the point is that it can always be found. Hence, none of the items in the world of our experience can be really or truly F—F in a way that excludes ever, in any way, being the opposite. But we do have a grasp of what it is for something to be really and truly

F, for this is what we grasp when we understand what it is to be F. So we find that the objects of our understanding are not the items in the world of our experience, which can always turn out to be the opposite of F as well as F, but rather "the F itself," the Form which we grasp in thought when we understand what it is to be F.

This argument shows why Plato connects the difference between being and coming to be so closely to the difference between knowledge and belief. It also gives a role to his emphasis on change, since a thing's changing is clearly one way in which it can turn out to be F from one perspective and the opposite of F from another. What has caused most difficulty is that the argument from opposites will produce Forms, obviously, only for terms with opposites, but that, while Plato sometimes appears to realize (and indeed build on) this, at other times he expands the "range" of Forms without argument.

This problem is one of the many that we are left with, along with Plato's own six objections, when we try to bring together all his views on Forms. Plato does not pretend to have a final version. He makes a respected older philosopher say to Socrates, in the *Parmenides*, that the further work the theory needs is to be found in the practice of argument, and this is doubtless Plato's advice to us.

· · · · ·

A FAMOUS IMAGE OF PLATO

One of the most famous and often-reproduced images of Plato comes from Raphael's fresco *The School of Athens*, painted for the

Pictured is the center detail of Plato and Aristotle from Raphael's fresco *The School of Athens* (1509–10), which is in the Room of the Segnatura at the Vatican.

This detail of St. Justin Martyr is from Raphael's fresco *Disputation over the Sacrament* (1509–10), which appears on the wall opposite *The School of Athens* in the Room of the Segnatura at the Vatican.

library of Pope Julius II. This picture of ancient philosophy is heavily influenced by the revival of Platonism in the Renaissance, and dominated by the figures of Plato, who holds the *Timaeus* and points upward, while Aristotle, holding his *Ethics*, looks at Plato's upraised hand but also gestures outward. The contrasting gestures indicate that Aristotle is more concerned to understand the world around us in terms of philosophical principles, while

Plato is more austerely focused on the abstract and theoretical principles themselves. In the fresco there is great stress on the *Timaeus'* mathematization of the world's underlying structure. Plato is shown between Pythagoras and Euclid, and his features are not those of the ancient portrait busts, but those of a contemporary mathematician, Leonardo da Vinci. In the Renaissance, Plato was also important as the philosopher most influential on Christianity. On the wall opposite, Raphael's depiction of the Trinity is greatly influenced by contemporary Neoplatonic writers. Saint Justin, a Platonist philosopher of the second century CE, who converted to Christianity and was martyred, repeats Plato's upward gesture as he points toward the Incarnation. In Pope Julius's scheme, the highest achievement of pagan philosophy recurs on a reduced scale in the representation of the central ideas of Christianity.

· · · · ·

Conclusion: Philosophy

The Japanese Plato scholar Noburu Notomi has pointed out that when Western philosophy was introduced to Japan in the nineteenth century, a new word ("tetsu-gaku") was coined for it, for, although the various branches of what we call philosophy (cosmology, logic, moral and political thought, for example) had been extensively developed in Eastern intellectual traditions, these studies had not been unified under the heading of "philosophy." They have not always been unified in Western intellectual traditions either, and Notomi is in good company in finding Plato to be the first thinker for whom philosophy is a unified endeavor, to be defined and defended against competitors as being the way for us to seek understanding and wisdom. Plato was the first to institutionalize philosophy (giving us the word "Academy") and to think of it as requiring both a systematic pursuit of truth and a radical dependence on argument, with others and with oneself. It is not surprising that he left a divided legacy of dogmatists and skeptical inquirers, or that his dialogues have lent themselves, over two thousand years, to the most divergent interpretations. For in the end, his deepest message is not that we should believe in Forms, or the importance of virtue, but that we should engage with him, and with our own contemporaries, in aspiring to understand these matters.

Although the various branches of what we call philosophy had been extensively developed in Eastern intellectual thought, they were not gathered under the heading of "philosophy" until Western philosophy was introduced to Japan in the nineteenth century. However, the poetry of Kakinomoto no Hitomaro (ca. 658–ca. 708), who is shown in this color ukiyo-e print, exemplifies a Shinto esthetic in which what we now recognize as the various branches of philosophy are brought together.

あしびきの山鳥の尾のしだり尾の

ながながし夜をひとりかも寝ん

柿本人麿

REFERENCES

•

CHAPTER 1

The issue discussed in connection with the jury passage in the *Theaetetus* was first clearly raised, and its importance stressed, by Myles Burnyeat in "Socrates and the Jury: Paradoxes in Plato's Distinction Between Knowledge and True Belief," *Aristotelian Society* Supplementary Volume LIV (1980), 173–91.

CHAPTER 2

Alice Riginos, in *Platonica*, the anecdotes concerning the life and writings of Plato (Brill, Leiden, 1976) shows the fragility of the ancient traditions about Plato. (See pp. 64–69 for Egypt stories; pp. 9–32 for Plato's "Apollonian nature"; pp. 35–40 for Plato's name; and pp. 70–85 for Plato's political involvements.) For details about Plato's family, see J. K. Davies, *Athenian Propertied Families* (Oxford University Press, 1971). For Socrates, see C. C. W. Taylor, *Socrates*, in the Oxford University Press Very Short Introduction series, and also the articles in Paul Vander Waerdt (ed.), *The Socratic Tradition* (Cornell University Press, 1994).

CHAPTER 3

See Andrea Nightingale, *Genres in Dialogue: Plato and the Construct of Philosophy* (Cambridge University Press, 1995), for Plato's demarcation of philosophy from other literary genres.

The Anonymous Commentator on the *Theaetetus* (quoted at column 54, 38–43) is a dogmatic Platonist who here records the position of the skeptical Academics. His date is uncertain, and may be from the first century BCE to the second CE. Plutarch of Chaeronea is a second-century CE dogmatic Platonist writer, best known for his historical biographies, who has sympathy for the skeptical tradition. The quotation from Cicero is from *Academica* II 46; that from Sextus is from *Outlines of Scepticism* I 221–23.

For an introduction to "Atlantis studies," see Richard Ellis, *Imagining Atlantis* (New York, Random House, 1998).

CHAPTER 4

For Augustine, see *City of God*, Book VIII, especially Chapter 5. Serious recent study of ancient homosexuality begins with K. J. Dover's *Greek Homosexuality* (London, Duckworth, 1978). For an up-to-date discussion, see James Davidson, *Courtesans and Fishcakes: The Consuming Passions of Ancient Athens* (London, Fontana, 1998).

Tom Stoppard's *The Invention of Love* is published by Grove Press, New York (1997).

CHAPTER 5

Plato's assumptions about happiness are clear in the *Euthydemus* and *Philebus*, though he does not lay them out explicitly as his pupil

Aristotle was to do in his *Nicomachean Ethics*. The *Euthydemus* is the major passage in which Plato develops the idea that it is the use of things that matters, and that they don't have value in themselves; a modified version of this can be found in the first two books of the *Laws*. *Apology*, *Crito*, and *Gorgias* are the major sources for Socrates' uncompromising commitment to the position that virtue is sufficient for happiness. Plato's views about education and the relation of the individual to community and to political society are to be found in the *Statesman* and *Laws*, as well as the more familiar *Republic*, whose "ideal state" has been read in a literal-minded way, and overemphasized, by many interpreters.

CHAPTER 6

Plato's arguments about the soul can best be encountered in the *Phaedo*, *Republic*, *Phaedrus*, and *Laws*. A collection of recent articles which forms a good introduction to the major issues is *Essays on Plato's Psychology*, edited by Ellen Wagner (Lexington Books, 2001).

CHAPTER 7

Plato's difficult dialogue *Timaeus* is translated with a long introduction by Donald Zeyl (Hackett, Indianapolis, 2000). A short introduction to important issues in Plato's approach to cosmology is Gregory Vlastos, *Plato's Universe* (Oxford University Press, 1975). Arguments about Forms, and about knowledge, are treated in papers reprinted in Gail Fine (ed.), *Plato* I (Oxford University Press, 2000). Plato's metaphysics and epistemology are the subject of much of the introductory literature mentioned under "Further Reading."

The comment by Noburu Notomi is from the introduction to his book *The Unity of Plato's Sophist* (Cambridge University Press, 1999). In my *Ancient Philosophy: A Very Short Introduction*, Chapter 6, I say a little more about philosophy in the ancient world and about Plato's role as establishing philosophy as a subject.

FURTHER READING

•

There are now available many recent translations of all of Plato's dialogues. The complete works are available in *Plato, Complete Dialogues*, edited by John Cooper (Hackett, 1997). Several dialogues are also available in individual Hackett translations, and also in recent translations published by Penguin and in the Oxford World's Classics series. Individual dialogues are all available in inexpensive paperback editions. If you become interested in Plato, you are well advised to read a dialogue in several translations, to get some idea of difficulties in the text.

The Clarendon Plato series contains new translations accompanied by philosophical commentary; these are for someone with a more advanced interest.

Several recent collections highlight problems of method in reading Plato, including Charles Kahn, *Plato and the Socratic Dialogue* (Cambridge University Press, 1996); C. Gill and M. M. McCabe (eds.), *Form and Argument in Later Plato* (Oxford University Press, 1996); J. C. Klagge and N. D. Smith (eds.), *Methods of Interpreting Plato and His Dialogues*, *Oxford Studies in Ancient Philosophy* Supplementary Volume, 1992; J. Annas and C. J. Rowe (eds.), *New Perspectives on Plato, Modern and Ancient* (Harvard University Press, 2002).

There are many short introductions to Plato in standard reference works. (The articles on Plato in the new *Oxford Classical Dictionary* and in *Greek Thought: A Guide to Classical Knowledge* by Harvard University Press were written by me.)

Richard Kraut (ed.), *Cambridge Companion to Plato* is a useful introduction to various aspects of Plato and has good bibliographies, both on individual dialogues and on Platonic topics. Christopher Rowe's *Plato* is a good medium-length survey. Christopher Gill, *Greek Thought*, is excellent background to Plato's ethical and social thought. Gail Fine, *On Ideas*, is a thorough examination of the arguments for Forms and Aristotle's criticisms of them.

INDEX

•

Page numbers in *italics* include illustrations and photographs/captions.

PICTURE CREDITS

•

LC-USZ62-66266; 100: LC-USZC4-10049; 102: LC-USZ62-42033; 119: LC-USZC2-2588; 126: LC-USZ62-98765; 132: LC-USZ62-105997; 134: LC-USZ62-95177; 151: LC-DIG-jpd-01964; 152–53: LC-USZC4-9704

COURTESY OF RARE BOOK AND SPECIAL COLLECTIONS DIVISION, LIBRARY OF CONGRESS: 124: Illustration from William Blake, *Europe: A Prophecy* (1794)

SHUTTERSTOCK: 9: © Shutterstock/Ela Kwasniewski; 40: © Shutterstock/ Christos Georghiou; 45: © Shutterstock/Igor Kisselev; 57: © Shutterstock/ Techlogica; 113: © Shutterstock/Morphart

COURTESY OF WIKIMEDIA COMMONS: 3: Meister des al-Mubashshir-Manuskripts, *Socrates and Two Students*/Yorck Project: 10.000 Meisterwerke der Malerei; 7: Jean-Léon Gérôme, *Phryne Before the Areopagus* (1861); 13: Illustration at the beginning of Euclid's *Elementa* (1309–16), in the translation attributed to Adelard of Bath; 15: *Euclid, or the Architecture* (1334–36) by Nino Pisano/Upload by Jastrow; 19: Meister des al-Mubashshir-Manuskripts, *Solon and Students*/Yorck Project: 10.000 Meisterwerke der Malerei; 22: Triad statue of pharaoh Menkaura, Hathor, and the personification of the nome of Diospolis Parva/Upload by Chipdawes; 23: *Eirene Bearing Plutus*/Upload by Bibi Saint-Pol; 25: Pompeo Batoni, *Apollo and Two Muses* (1741); 27: Bust of Socrates/Upload by Jastrow; 34: Bust of Aristotle from the Ludovisi Collection at the Palazzo Altemps (Museo Nazionale Romano), Rome, Italy/Upload by Jastrow; 43: Plato in the *Nuremberg Chronicle*; 47: Reinhold Begas, *Kriegswissenschaft* (1887)/Upload by Mutter Erde; 52: Plato's Academy archaeological site in Akadimia Platonos subdivision of Athens, Greece/Upload by Tomisti; 53: Plotinus in the *Nuremberg Chronicle*/Upload by Zp at cs.wikipedia, transferred by Sevela.p; 55: Marcus Tullius Cicero, by Bertel Thorvaldsen, copy from Roman original/Upload by Gunnar Bach Pedersen; 59: Actor wearing the mask of a rustic from Canino, Italy/Upload by Jastrow; 60: Oxyrhynchus Papyrus, containing excerpts from *The Republic*; 61: Rembrandt, *Homer*/ Yorck Project: 10.000 Meisterwerke der Malerei; 65: Parthenon/Upload by Thermos; 66: *Erastes* (lover) and *eromenos* (beloved) kissing/Upload by Jastrow; 69: Alcibiades, Palazzo dei Conservatori, Hall of the Triumphs / Upload by Jastrow; 70: Anselm Feuerbach, *Plato's Symposium*/Yorck Project: 10.000 Meisterwerke der Malerei; 73: Woman grinding wheat/Upload by Jastrow; 84: Raphael, detail, tondo of Justice in the Room of the Segnatura in the Vatican/Yorck Project: 10.000 Meisterwerke der Malerei; 85: Zeno of Citium/Upload by Shakko; 87: *Virtuous Woman Tames Woodwose* from *Zahm und wild, Basler und Straßburger Bildteppiche des 15. Jahrhunderts*; 91: Landscape scene from the *Odyssey* by a Roman master, ca. 60–40 BCE/Yorck Project: 10.000 Meisterwerke der Malerei; 92: Statue of Melpomene, muse of tragedy (second century CE) from Monte Calvo/Upload by Wolfgang Sauber; 95: Family scene with inscription "[daughter of] Mousiaos," Musée du Louvre/Upload by Jastrow; 97: Kleroterion/Upload by Xocolatl; 98: Pinakia/Upload by Marsyas; 99: Pnyx/Upload by Qwqchris; 106l: Statue of Pothos/Upload by Jastrow; 106r: Statue of Athena/Upload by Jastrow; 109: Image of *Timaeus* pages from 1578 Stephanus edition of Plato's works; 110: Mark Antokolski, *Death of Socrates* (1875)/Upload by Alex Bakharev; 115: Jan Saenredam, *Taste*; 117: Aristotle in the *Nuremberg Chronicle*; 121: Wheel of reincarnation/Upload by Calton; 128: Albrecht Dürer, *Salvator Mundi* (1504)/Yorck Project: 10.000 Meisterwerke der Malerei; 130–31: Sculpture of Actaeon, Royal Palace at Caserta/Upload by Japiot; 138: Monfredo de Monte Imperiali, *Liber de herbis, Imaginary Debate Between Averroes and Porphyry*; 144–45: Sandro Botticelli, Frescoes from the Villa Lemmi near Florence, scene: Giovanna degli Albizi with Venus and the Graces, fragment/Yorck Project: 10.000 Meisterwerke der Malerei; 148: Raphael, *Disputation over the Sacrament*, detail/Yorck Project: 10.000 Meisterwerke der Malerei

BRIEF INSIGHTS

•

A series of concise, engrossing, and enlightening books that explore
every subject under the sun with unique insight.

Available now:

THE AMERICAN PRESIDENCY
Charles O. Jones

JUDAISM
Norman Solomon

ATHEISM
Julian Baggini

LITERARY THEORY
Jonathan Culler

BUDDHISM
Damien Keown

MODERN CHINA
Rana Mitter

THE CRUSADES
Christopher Tyerman

PAUL
E. P. Sanders

EXISTENTIALISM
Thomas Flynn

PHILOSOPHY
Edward Craig

HISTORY
John H. Arnold

PLATO
Julia Annas

• • • • •